Coronation Knits

by Susan Crawford

Susan Crawford Vintage

Editor: Susan Crawford
Creative Director: Susan Crawford
Photography: Susan Crawford
Styling, Hair & Make Up: Susan Crawford
Technical Editing: Jen Arnall-Culliford
Charts & Schematic Diagrams: Jen Arnall-Culliford
Book Design: Gavin Crawford
Artwork, & Graphic Design: Gavin Crawford
Models: Charlie Moon and Denis Brice

British Library Cataloguing-in-Publication Data
A catalogue record fro this book is available from the British Library

ISBN 978-0-9572286-0-3

First edition: June, 2012

Printed and bound in the UK
by The Lavenham Press Ltd
www.lavenhampress.com

First published in the UK by Susan Crawford Vintage

MIX
Paper from
responsible sources
FSC® C010693

Printed on FSC paper using
vegetable oil based inks.

"Designed, Knitted
and Made in Britain"

Made in
Britain

Susan Crawford Vintage

www.susancrawfordvintage.com

This book is dedicated to my mum, Lorna,
whose treasured scrapbook from many years ago
planted a seed that eventually became Coronation Knits.

ACKNOWLEDGEMENTS

I am privileged to have the assistance and support of a number of great knitters, Dorothy Crawford, my mother in law, who knits for me endlessly, Natascha Mozley and Bev Robinson and last but by no means least, Tom van Deijnen, who made the impossible happen by knitting the stole on the cover of the book in only three and a half days.

I must also thank my daughter Charlie who travelled from Edinburgh to Southport just to be my model and also Denis Brice who completely entered into the spirit of the project.

I would also like to thank Susan Hayward whose fabulous vintage shop in Southport has provided many of the period items seen on these pages and Julie Nelson Rhodes who generously loaned me an original 1953 Coronation commemorative scarf worn with the Crowning Glory beret and the Coronation Sleeveless Pullover, along with all the splendid yarn companies who have been so supportive towards this project.

Finally I would like to thank Jen Arnall Culliford, my intrepid tech editor who helps make my design ideas a reality and Kate Long for organising me and working on as many disparate things as I could manage to throw at her.

Contents

Introduction

Little did I realise, when I used to sit in my nan and granddad's back kitchen on rainy Sunday afternoons looking through my mum's old scrapbooks, that one of them would be such an influence on me that I would put a book together around it. Yet here we are. The scrapbook itself is unfortunately no more. When we came to clear out my grandparent's house in the mid 1990s, it was nowhere to be found. But even though I can no longer physically turn its pages, I can remember so much of its contents. Mum collected every newspaper cutting that she could find about Elizabeth II but particularly, photographs of her in outfits that my mum really liked. I only really appreciated how close their style was when I found a photograph of the Queen in an old book in a coat almost identical to one worn by my mum around the same time.

I've always talked at length about the influences my grandmothers had on me and as a result of that my mum probably gets overlooked. But it was my mum who kept all of her Photoplay film annuals from the 1950s which I poured over week after week, year after year and mum who kept scrapbooks of subjects such as the Queen and the Coronation.

The idea of creating a book around the Coronation began to germinate last autumn, but as I was still in the process of working on A Stitch in Time, volume 2, it had to wait for a quiet period at the beginning of this year, for a chance to resurface and gain momentum. The concept was to design a collection with a common theme – the Coronation and the years around it and Elizabeth's role as a style icon – that together make a strong, coherent collection, but which also work just as well individually. Both charts and written instructions are given where-ever possible and some designs have instructions for both flat and circular construction, making the book accessible to knitters of differing persuasions!

I love each and every design in the book and would find it almost impossible to pick a favourite and sincerely hope that they will appeal to everyone who has been kind enough to purchase a copy – and not just for the Diamond Jubilee but for a long time to come.

Susan

History

In February 1952, King George VI unexpectedly passed away and an unprepared 26 year old Princess Elizabeth ascended the throne. My mother was twelve years old at the time and had already been collecting newspapers cuttings about the princesses, Elizabeth and Margaret for some time. These cuttings were stuck into her Royal Family scrap book. Along with film stars of the day, the princesses were my mum's fashion icons, their apparently glamorous lives, viewed only at the cinema or in the daily newspaper, transported her into another world. Elizabeth's personal style was emulated by my mum for several years, even down to her hairstyle and mum has continued to follow her life in the papers and on television.

The Coronation in June 1953 provided excitement and colour in a Britain that was still caught in the throes of post war austerity. Many cities remained derelict and in disrepair

from war damage as the country struggled financially, due to crippling loan repayments to the US and a lack of economic growth. Extreme austerity measures heightened by the continuation of rationing left many families struggling as much as they had done during WWII. Petrol rationing was removed in 1950 but this wasn't enough to save the incumbent Labour government who lost narrowly to the Conservatives in October 1951. The Festival of Britain held in the same year did not lift the country's spirits sufficiently to prevent a change of political heart. In 1952 tea rationing finally ended with sweet rationing ceasing in February 1953. Meat wasn't taken off ration however until July 1954 along with any other remaining food items.

Clothes rationing had ended in 1949 and although there was great controversy in Britain over the 'New Look' from Christian Dior and its extravagant use of fabric and trimmings, women were desperate for colour and glamour in their lives. Skirts and dresses became fuller and longer and jumpers and cardigans extended past the waist to the hip. Bat-wing sleeves were 'the' fashion statement using significantly more yarn or fabric than previously. Buttons appeared in profusion on cardigans, increasing from two or three to ten, eleven, or even twelve. Garments both knitted or sewn were decorated with beads or sequins for added elegance. Underwear altered dramatically to further enhance the new hourglass shape, with bullet bras lifting the bust-line higher than in the previous two decades and waist hugging girdles nipping the waist in to almost unbelievable proportions. Elasticated belts were worn tight to emphasise this curvy shape even more. At the same time, the influence of sportswear from the US began to take effect, creating a longer line with a looser more relaxed fit than seen before. This more casual look was adopted by the youth of the 1950s – the new social group known as teenagers. No longer happy to dress the same as their parents, teenagers began to create their own style which even influenced hand knitting.

The hand knitting market in the UK was dominated by companies such as Sirdar, Patons, Lavenda and Wendy, with a single pattern leaflet often selling over 20,000 copies. Yarn was suddenly available in a kaleidoscope of colours opening up a whole new era for enthusiastic knitters – knitting for pleasure rather than purely for economy or make do and mend. At least one knitting shop could be found in almost every town or city, offering a wide range of yarns and patterns. These patterns were usually written for flat construction – separate pieces which were then sewn together. This style of pattern writing had started in the 1930s and remained the most popular method of writing instructions right through the 1950s and beyond. Although patterns remained predominantly single sized, multi sized patterns began to appear with increasing regularity at this time – although 'outsize' or 'matron' sizing still began with a 38 inch bust!

Stitchcraft and their direct competitor Needlework Illustrated provided monthly magazines packed with all manner of crafting projects. A personal favourite of mine, Pins and Needles, offered step by step instruction on everything from a hand knitted bolero to building a set of bedroom furniture in a weekend. Woman's Weekly continued to promote its knitting patterns heavily with it often appearing as the main cover image, in the knowledge that knitters were eagerly awaiting the latest design. Stitchcraft, Needlework Illustrated etc., promoted a vision of the domestic goddess who could knit, sew, embroider, cook and build a coffee table – all whilst looking serene, beautiful and perfectly dressed and of course, putting her husband first – quite a tall order! Women in 1950s Britain usually stopped work upon marriage, certainly upon having children, yet during WWII many women, married or otherwise, worked in previously male dominated occupations. After the war, women were actively encouraged to return to a purely domestic role in the household, with women's magazines playing a major role in exerting this influence. It therefore seems wonderfully ironic that the new monarch was a married, working woman and mother.

On 2nd June 1953, the Coronation of Queen Elizabeth II took place. My mum and her family went several doors down the street to watch the ceremony on a neighbour's new television set. At this point, they didn't own their own. This was then followed by a huge street party for neighbours, family and friends. Photographs look remarkably similar to the 'Victory' party held a few years earlier – almost as though time had stood still.

Britain has changed dramatically since 1953 and yet there are so many parallels and similarities between then and now: Austerity, economic upheaval, a recent change of government, media influence, even two major events in a short space of time – The Festival of Britain and the Coronation in the 1950s, the Diamond Jubilee and the Olympics in 2012. Add to that a recent royal wedding and the rise of the former Kate Middleton as a style icon exactly as happened to Elizabeth after her wedding to Philip and just like fashion, history certainly does seem to be repeating itself!

Suggested Reading

Austerity Britain 1945-1951 — David Kynaston : Bloomsbury, 2007
Family Britain 1951-1957 — David Kynaston : Bloomsbury, 2010
Nella Last in the 1950s — Patricia & Robert Malcolmson : Profile Books, 2010
The Coronation Book of Queen Elizabeth II — Odhams Press, 1953

This book is not a learn to knit book, so some prior knowledge of basic knitting techniques is required. Below are some of the more specific techniques, used in some of the patterns in the book along with some basic information to help you get the best from the patterns.

Tension or Gauge squares

I won't labour the point here but it is vitally important to knit a tension square before commencing knitting the full project to ensure that your tension exactly matches that of the knitter of the original sample piece. The slightest difference in tension can result in an ill fitting garment and a disappointing final result.

Sizing Information

Before starting to knit please carefully check the comprehensive sizing information supplied for each pattern to help you decide which size to knit. The 'To Fit' measurement is the size of the intended wearer, and the measurements following are those of the finished project if the pattern is knitted exactly and tension is correct. The amount of ease and adjustments for size have already been made to the pattern based on my own standard sizing chart. However it is at this point that you have the opportunity to make adjustments if necessary. (For more information about getting a customised fit see A Stitch in Time, Vintage Knitting patterns, Vol 2). Where appropriate it is also stated which size garment is being shown in any photographs. Charlie, the female model throughout, is styled in 1950s underwear and is wearing a bullet bra and girdle to create a very 1950s silhouette. It is not necessary to wear this style of underwear for the garments to fit correctly but you certainly can if you wish!

Negative Ease

Some of the patterns in the book are written to be worn with negative ease. This means that the garment is smaller than the intended wearer and that it is designed to be stretched over the body. You will see this on the sizing chart on the finished bust measurements. This ease is taken into account in the pattern and it is important that you still use the correct 'To fit' measurement to get the intended fit.

Casting On

Unless otherwise stated I usually use cable cast on for the projects in this book and the instructions are therefore written with this cast on as the starting point for all the patterns. If you prefer to use a different cast on please bear this in mind when commencing to knit. Cable cast on is simply placing your right hand needle behind the last st cast on, working as though to knit but placing the loop of the stitch onto the left hand needle.

Fair Isle / Intarsia Combination Colour Work

Patterns of this period often used this combination of both colour work techniques, carrying colours across single motifs or small areas but not from one motif or section to the next, instead using separate small balls of yarn for each of these sections. This is so that large areas between motifs do not have yarn being carried across work and ensuring that the project remains single thickness. It is important to ensure when moving on to the next section that yarns are crossed over each other at the back of the work to prevent holes. Within each section yarns are stranded at the back of the work as in fair Isle. Lion and Unicorn jumper uses this combination technique.

Three Needle Cast Off

This method involves leaving the required shoulder stitches on a needle so that they can be knitted together with the matching shoulder stitches from a second piece of knitting. To do this, hold both needles in your left hand with work RS together. Insert a third needle of about the same size into the first stitch of each needle in your left hand and knit these two stitches together. Repeat the process with the next two stitches then cast the resulting first stitch off over the second. Continue in this way until all stitches have been cast off.

w&t (Wrap and Turn)

Some of the patterns in the book use short row shaping in conjunction with wrap and turns. A w&t as it is known is performed on the first un-worked stitch next to a set of short row stitches to prevent steps appearing in the work. The method used most commonly in the book is worked as follows:

Work the number of stitches specified in the pattern, then slip the next stitch on to the right hand needle, then bring the yarn to the opposite side of the work to where it is sitting. Pass the slipped stitch back onto the left needle then turn the work round. The yarn will be at the wrong side of the work to work your next stitch, so again take it to the opposite side of the work from where it is sitting behind the un-worked stitch, then work the following stitch, on the LH needle. On the next or a subsequent row, you will work across the wrapped sts and it is essential you knit or purl the wrap together with the stitch it is wrapped around to avoid an ugly stitch.

On a knit row: Put right needle through wrap at front of work as though to knit, then put needle through wrapped stitch also knitwise, now knit the wrap and the stitch together.

On a purl row: Put right needle through wrap from back of work as though to purl, then put needle through wrapped st also from back of work, purlwise, then purl the wrap and the stitch together.

Slipped Yarnover (known as slyo)

This method of turning is used in the Retro Jubilee Socks and is an alternative way to prevent a step in the work and also to prevent a hole:

After turning work, bring yarn to the front as though to purl. With right needle, slip the next stitch purlwise. Take the yarn over the top of the right hand needle to the back of the work, pulling tightly so that both 'legs' of the stitch below are stretched over the needle.

If on a RS row the yarn is already in correct position to K the next st.

If on a WS row bring the yarn to the front of work before working the next st.

After working a slyo it will be necessary on a subsequent row to work the slyo. To do so, insert the right needle under BOTH legs of the st and and either K or P together depending on which side of work you are on. It is important that the slyo is not mistaken for two separate stitches as this would result in an increased st if they are worked separately.

Finishing

Instructions are given at the end of each pattern on how to 'finish' the project appropriately including how to press or block your finished project.

Buttonhole stitch

Buttonhole stitch is worked from left to right. Hold thread with thumb and put needle through the fabric at right angles to the direction of the thread. Draw the needle through over the thread, still holding the thread in position with your thumb. Pull up the thread to crate a bar along the buttonhole edge. Continue in this manner until you have worked right around buttonhole and fasten off securely on WS of work.

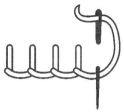

Button Loops

A crocheted button loop is basically a crochet chain attached to your knitting. To make a button loop using a crochet hook, insert hook through work in required position, from front to back. Draw yarn through onto hook. Grab yarn with the hook and draw through the stitch already on the hook. Repeat until loop is long enough when stretched to go round button. Attach remaining end of loop by inserting hook through knitting, bring yarn around hook and draw through. Cut the yarn and bring through loop and fasten off securely.

Resources

Yarns

Belle – Juno Fibre Arts – www.etsy.com/shop/JunoFibreArts
Excelana Luxury 4 Ply wool – Susan Crawford Vintage Yarns – www.susancrawfordvintage.com
Organic Poll Dorset 4 ply – Renaissance Dyeing – www.renaissancedyeing.com
Tempo 4 ply – Eden Cottage Yarns – edencottageyarns.co.uk
4 ply Lambswool – J C Rennie – www.knitrennie.co.uk
2 ply Jumper weight Shetland wool – Jamieson & Smith – www.shetlandwoolbrokers.co.uk
Cygnet Truly Wool Rich 4 ply – Cygnet Yarns – www.cygnetyarns.com
Scrumptious Lace – Fyberspates – www.fyberspates.co.uk
Semi Precious DK – babylonglegs – babylonglegs.bigcartel.com

Clothing

Female model's underwear from What Katie Did – www.whatkatiedid.com
Vintage clothing and props – author's own or from Susan Hayward, 16 Post Office Avenue, Southport 01704 545567

Diamonds are Forever

MATERIALS
Renaissance Dyeing Poll Dorset 100% organic wool
(350m / 380yds per 100g skein)
3 (4, 4, 5, 5, 6, 6) skeins, shade Pastel – MC
1 skein shade Midi – CC
1 skein shade Puivert – A
1 skein shade Carmine – B
1 skein shade Ecru – C
1 2.75mm (US #2) circular needle
A set of 2.75mm (US #2) double pointed needles (DPNs)
1 3.25mm (US #3) circular needle
A set of 3.25mm (US #3) DPNs
Stitch markers
Stitch holders

TENSION
30 sts & 38 rows = 10cm (4in) using 3.25mm needles over
stocking stitch in the round

ABBREVIATIONS
See page 95

SIZING

To Fit	cm	76–81	86	91	97	101	107–112	117–122
	(in)	(30–32)	(34)	(36)	(38)	(40)	(42–44)	(48–50)
Actual Bust Size	cm	84	89½	94½	100	108	118½	129½
	(in)	(33)	(35¼)	(37¼)	(39¼)	(42½)	(46¾)	(51)
Length to Underarm	cm	34½	35½	36½	38	39½	40½	41½
	(in)	(13½)	(14)	(14¼)	(15)	(15½)	(16)	(16¼)
Yoke Depth	cm	18	19½	22	23	23½	25	26½
	(in)	(7¼)	(7¾)	(8½)	(9)	(9¼)	(9¾)	(10¼)
Finished Length	cm	52½	55	58½	61	63	65½	68
	(in)	(20¾)	(21¾)	(23)	(24)	(25)	(25¾)	(26¾)
Sleeve Length	cm	38	41	41	42	42	43	43
	(in)	(15)	(16¼)	(16¼)	(16½)	(16½)	(17)	(17)

Model is shown wearing size to fit chest 76–81cm (30–32in)

PATTERN NOTES
This pattern is worked in the round from the
bottom up in stocking stitch, so every round is
knitted, unless otherwise stated.

BODY
Using yarn CC and 2.75mm circular needle, cast on
252 (268, 284, 300, 324, 356, 388) sts, placing a
marker after 126 (134, 142, 150, 162, 178, 194)
sts. Join into a round, taking care not to twist sts
and place a marker at join to mark right side seam.
Change to MC and work in rib as folls:
Next round (RS): * K1, P1, rep from * to end.
Rep this round until rib measures 2½cm (1in) from
cast on edge.
Change to 3.25mm needle and work in stocking
stitch (every round K) for 25 rounds. (Work should
measure 9cm (3½in)).

Rep the last 16 (18, 18, 20, 20, 22, 22) rounds once more, 252 (268, 284, 300, 324, 356, 388) sts.

Work without further shaping until body measures 34½ (35½, 36½, 38, 39½, 40½, 41½) cm (13½, 14, 14½, 15, 15½, 16, 16½ in), ending last round 9 sts before end of round marker. Transfer last 9 sts before marker, and first 9 sts after marker onto waste yarn or a stitch holder, leaving rem 234 (250, 266, 282, 306, 338, 370) sts on spare needle. Leave to one side.

SLEEVES

Using yarn CC and 2.75mm double pointed needles, cast on 62 (64, 70, 70, 72, 74, 76) sts. Join into a round, taking care not to twist sts and place a marker at join to mark end of round.

Change to MC and work in rib as folls:
Next round (RS): * K1, P1, rep from * to end.
Rep this round until rib measures 5cm (2in) from cast on edge.
Change to 3.25mm double pointed needles and K 3 rounds.

Shape Body

Next round (Dec): K4, K2tog, K to 6 sts before side marker, SSK, K4, SM, K4, K2tog, K to last 6 sts of round, SSK, K4, 248 (264, 280, 296, 320, 352, 384) sts.

Work 15 (17, 17, 19, 19, 21, 21) rounds straight, then work dec round once more, 244 (260, 276, 292, 316, 348, 380) sts.
Rep the last 16 (18, 18, 20, 20, 22, 22) rounds once more, 240 (256, 272, 288, 312, 344, 376) sts rem. Work without further shaping for 10 rounds.

Next round (Inc): K4, M1, K to last 4 sts before side marker, M1, K4, SM, K4, M1, K to last 4 sts of round, M1, K4, 244 (260, 276, 292, 316, 348, 380) sts.

Work 15 (17, 17, 19, 19, 21, 21) rounds straight, then work inc round once more, 248 (264, 280, 296, 320, 352, 384) sts.

Inc 1 st at beg and end of next and 6 (3, 3, 13, 1, 9, 1) foll 12th (13th, 13th, 9th, 7th, 6th, 5th) rounds, 76 (72, 78, 98, 76, 94, 80) sts. Inc 1 st at beg and end of 3 (6, 6, 1, 15, 11, 21) foll 13th (14th, 14th, 10th, 8th, 7th, 6th) rounds, 82 (84, 90, 100, 106, 116, 122) sts.

Continue without further shaping until sleeve measures 38 (41, 41, 42, 42, 43, 43) cm (15, 16, 16, 16½, 16½, 17, 17 in) ending 9 sts before marker on last round. Transfer last 9 sts before marker, and first 9 sts after marker onto waste yarn or a stitch holder, leaving rem 64 (66, 72, 82, 88, 98, 104) sts on a spare needle.

Join for Yoke

Using yarn MC and 3.25mm circular needle, K across 64 (66, 72, 82, 88, 98, 104) sts on one sleeve, PM, K across 108 (116, 124, 132, 144, 160, 176) sts for front, PM, ending 9 sts before side seam marker. Place next 18 body sts on holder or waste yarn, K across 64 (66, 72, 82, 88, 98, 104) sts from second sleeve, PM, and K across rem 108 (116, 124, 132, 144, 160, 176) sts for back. Place a different coloured marker to mark new beginning of round, 344 (364, 392, 428, 464, 516, 560) sts.

Raglan Shaping
Next round: * K2, K2tog, K to last 4 sts before next marker, SSK, K2, SM, rep from * to end of round (8 decs worked), 336 (356, 384, 420, 456, 508, 552) sts.

Next round: K.
Rep the last 2 rounds 9 (8, 8, 9, 8, 8, 8) times more, 264 (292, 320, 348, 392, 444, 488) sts rem, then K 0 (1, 2, 3, 4, 4, 5) rounds.

SET UP YOKE PATTERN
Next round: Knit, decreasing 2 (0, 2, 2, 2, 2, 2) sts evenly across first sleeve, dec 4 (2, 2, 4, 2, 4, 2) sts across front, dec 2 (0, 2, 2, 2, 2, 2) sts across second sleeve then dec 4 (2, 2, 4, 2, 4, 2) sts across back, 252 (288, 312, 336, 384, 432, 480) sts.

K 1 (2, 3, 5, 4, 4, 6) rounds.

Next round: Commencing with round 1 of chart and reading from right to left on all rounds, work chart across round 42 (48, 52, 56, 64, 72, 80) times.

Continue as set by previous round until all 30 rounds of chart have been worked.

Work in MC only from this point onwards.

K 1 (4, 7, 9, 10, 10, 12) rounds without further shaping.

Yoke Decreases
Next round (Dec): * K3 (3, 3, 3, 4, 4, 3), K2tog, rep from * to last 2 (3, 2, 1, 0, 0, 0) sts, K to end, 202 (231, 250, 269, 320, 360, 384) sts.

K 11 (13, 17, 15, 10, 13, 13) rounds without further shaping.

Next round (Dec): * K2 (2, 2, 2, 3, 3, 2), K2tog, rep from * to last 2 (3, 2, 1, 0, 0, 0) sts, K to end, 152 (174, 188, 202, 256, 288, 288) sts.

Chart

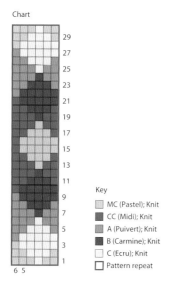

Key
- ▨ MC (Pastel); Knit
- ■ CC (Midi); Knit
- ▦ A (Puivert); Knit
- ■ B (Carmine); Knit
- □ C (Ecru); Knit
- □ Pattern repeat

6 5

5th, 6th and 7th sizes only

K (7, 9, 9) rounds.

Next round (Dec): K (6, 0, 6), * K (3, 2, 2), K2tog, rep from * to last (10, 0, 8) sts, K to end, (208, 216, 220) sts.

All sizes

K 2 rounds.

Change to 2.75mm circular needle and work in rib as folls:

Next round: * K1, P1, rep from * to end of round. Rep this row a further 9 times. Change to yarn CC and 3.25mm needle and cast off in rib loosely.

MAKING UP

Either graft or work a three needle cast off to join underarm and sleeve sts together.

Wash gently in lukewarm soapy water, rinse then dry off garment inside a clean towel removing as much excess water as possible. Pin out to required measurements and leave to dry. Gently steam the garment before completely dry taking care not to touch with the iron itself. If preferred place a damp cloth over the garment whilst steaming. Leave to dry completely. Darn in all ends.

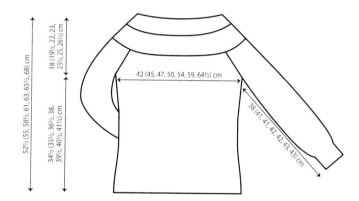

The concept of teenagers first came into existence in the 1950s alongside more casual, 'sports' wear from the US. Shetland knitwear was also experiencing a revival and in particular plain jumpers and cardigans with a fair isle yoke. I have always been a fan of this look and have a photograph of my mum as a teenager in capri pants, ballet pumps and a jumper worn clingingly tight over the bust and fitted at the waist to show off her newly acquired bullet bra. This type of jumper, albeit worn with very different undergarments, is very popular again today and I wanted to try and merge the two. Diamonds are forever is a simple garment, knitted in the round from the bottom up to the underarm. There is waist shaping to give the jumper a 50s silhouette. If preferred it can be knitted without the decreases and increases in the lower body to give a more unstructured shape. After the sleeves are knitted in the round up to the armhole the pieces are knitted together and the yoke worked. The diamond panel is a great introduction to Fair Isle techniques as it is a very simple pattern to follow. Any shaping in the yoke is worked either before or after the Fair Isle panel so this can be worked without any concerns about decreases. The neck is left wide with a slight boat neck appearance to complete the 1950's influence — There's more than a little of the young Brigitte Bardot to this fabulous jumper.

Crowning Glory

MATERIALS
Excelana 4 Ply Luxury Wool 100% pure new British wool
(159m / 174yds per 50g ball)
2 balls shade Alabaster
1 2.75mm (US #2) circular needle (length 40cm)
1 3mm (US #2–3) circular needle (length 40cm)
1 set 3mm (US 2–3) double pointed needles (DPNs)
Stitch markers

TENSION
28 sts & 36 rows = 10cm (4in) using 3mm needles
measured over stocking stitch

ABBREVIATIONS
See page 95

SIZING
52cm (21in) circumference measured after ribbing

To Fit Size		
cm	51½–57	
(in)	(20–22½)	

PATTERN NOTES
Both charted and written instructions are provided for this beret. The beret is knitted in the round from the
ribbing upwards.

BERET
Using 2.75mm circular needle, cast on 148 sts. Join
work into a round taking care not to twist stitches,
and commence working as folls:

Round 1: * K2, P2, rep from * to end of round.
Rep this round a further 7 times.
Next round (Inc): K4, * M1, K5, rep from * to last
4 sts, K4, 176 sts.
Next round: * K44, PM, rep from * to end of
round.
K 2 rounds.
Next round: * YO, K2tog, rep from * to end of
round.
K 4 rounds.
Next round: * K2tog, YO, rep from * to end of
round.

K 6 rounds.
Now follow either the charted or written
instructions to complete your beret.

CHARTED INSTRUCTIONS
Commencing with round 1, work from chart,
reading all rounds from right to left and working
pattern 4 times across round. Continue in this
manner working each round of chart as set, working
decreases either side of markers as shown and
changing to DPNs when necessary. When 24 sts
rem, break yarn leaving a long end, draw yarn
through rem sts and draw together firmly. Finish off
securely and darn in all ends.

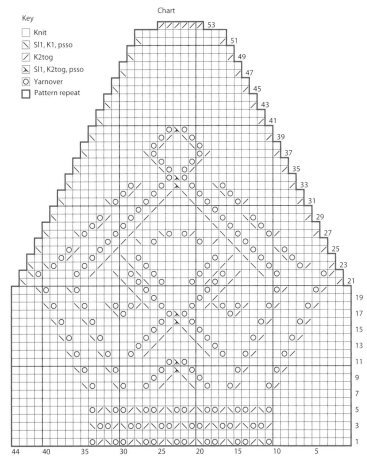

Chart

Key
- ☐ Knit
- ◣ Sl1, K1, psso
- ◢ K2tog
- ⊼ Sl1, K2tog, psso
- ○ Yarnover
- ☐ Pattern repeat

Round 11: [K21, YO, Sl1, K2tog, psso, YO, K20] 4 times.

Round 12: [K7, K2tog, YO, K3, K2tog, YO, K2, YO, K1, Sl1, K1, psso, K7, K2tog, K1, YO, K2, YO, Sl1, K1, psso, K2, YO, Sl1, K1, psso, K7] 4 times.

Round 13: [K17, YO, K1, Sl1, K1, psso, K5, K2tog, K1, YO, K16] 4 times.

Round 14: [K6, K2tog, YO, K3, K2tog, YO, K5, YO, K1, Sl1, K1, psso, K3, K2tog, K1, YO, K5, YO, Sl1, K1, psso, K2, YO, Sl1, K1, psso, K6] 4 times.

Round 15: [K19, YO, K1, Sl1, K1, psso, K1, K2tog, K1, YO, K18] 4 times.

Round 16: [K5, K2tog, YO, K3, K2tog, YO, K8, YO, K1, Sl1, K2tog, psso, K1, YO, K8, YO, Sl1, K1, psso, K2, YO, Sl1, K1, psso, K5] 4 times.

Round 17: [K14, K2tog, YO, K5, YO, Sl1, K2tog, psso, YO, K5, YO, Sl1, K1, psso, K13] 4 times.

Round 18: [K4, K2tog, YO, K3, K2tog, YO, K2, K2tog, YO, K1, YO, Sl1, K1, psso, K2tog, K1, YO, K3, YO, K1, Sl1, K1, psso, K2tog, YO, K1, YO, Sl1, K1, psso, K2, YO, Sl1, K1, psso, K2, YO, Sl1, K1, psso, K4] 4 times.

Round 19: [K17, K2tog, K1, YO, K5, YO, K1, Sl1, K1, psso, K16] 4 times.

Round 20: [K3, K2tog, YO, K3, K2tog, YO, K6, K2tog, K1, YO, K7, YO, K1, Sl1, K1, psso, K6, YO, Sl1, K1, psso, K2, YO, Sl1, K1, psso, K3] 4 times.

Shape Crown

Round 21 (Dec): [K2tog, K13, K2tog, K1, YO, K2tog, K1, YO, K3, YO, K1, Sl1, K1, psso, YO, K1, Sl1, K1, psso, K12, Sl1, K1, psso] 4 times, 168 sts.

Round 22: [K1, K2tog, YO, K5, YO, K1, Sl1, K1, psso, K2, K2tog, K1, YO, K2tog, K1, YO, K5, YO, K1, Sl1, K1, psso, YO, K1, Sl1, K1, psso, K2,

WRITTEN INSTRUCTIONS

Round 1: [K10, (YO, Sl1, K1, psso, K2tog, YO) 6 times, K10] 4 times.

Round 2: K.

Round 3: [K10, (K2tog, YO, YO, Sl1, K1, psso) 6 times, K10] 4 times.

Round 4: K.

Round 5: As round 1.

K 2 rounds.

Round 8: [K9, K2tog, YO, K3, K2tog, YO, K2, YO, K1, Sl1, K1, psso, K3, K2tog, K1, YO, K2, YO, Sl1, K1, psso, K2, YO, Sl1, K1, psso, K9] 4 times.

Round 9: [K19, YO, K1, Sl1, K1, psso, K1, K2tog, K1, YO, K18] 4 times.

Round 10: [K8, K2tog, YO, K3, K2tog, YO, K5, YO, K1, Sl1, K2tog, psso, K1, YO, K5, YO, Sl1, K1, psso, K2, YO, Sl1, K1, psso, K8] 4 times.

K2tog, K1, YO, K4, YO, Sl1, K1, psso, K1] 4 times.

Round 23 (Dec): [K2tog, K2, K2tog, YO, K3, YO, K1, Sl1, K1, psso, K3, K2tog, K1, YO, K7, YO, K1, Sl1, K1, psso, K3, K2tog, K1, YO, K3, YO, Sl1, K1, psso, K1, Sl1, K1, psso] 4 times, 160 sts.

Round 24: [K5, YO, Sl1, K1, psso, K2, YO, K1, Sl1, K1, psso, K1, K2tog, K1, YO, K9, YO, K1, Sl1, K1, psso, K1, K2tog, K1, YO, K2, K2tog, YO, K4] 4 times.

Round 25 (Dec): [K2tog, K4, YO, Sl1, K1, psso, K2, YO, K1, Sl1, K1, psso, K15, K2tog, K1, YO, K2, K2tog, YO, K3, Sl1, K1, psso] 4 times, 152 sts.

Round 26: [K10, YO, K1, Sl1, K1, psso, K1, K2tog, K1, YO, K5, YO, K1, Sl1, K1, psso, K1, K2tog, K1, YO, K9] 4 times.

Round 27 (Dec): [K2tog, K4, K2tog, YO, K3, YO, K1, Sl1, K1, psso, K3, K2tog, YO, K1, YO, Sl1, K1, psso, K3, K2tog, K1, YO, K3, YO, Sl1, K1, psso, K3, Sl1, K1, psso] 4 times, 144 sts.

Round 28: [K7, YO, Sl1, K1, psso, K2, YO, K1, Sl1, K1, psso, K9, K2tog, K1, YO, K2, K2tog, YO, K6] 4 times.

Round 29 (Dec): [K2tog, K6, YO, Sl1, K1, psso, K2, YO, K1, Sl1, K1, psso, K7, K2tog, K1, YO, K2, K2tog, YO, K5, Sl1, K1, psso] 4 times, 136 sts.

Round 30: [K12, YO, K1, Sl1, K1, psso, K5, K2tog, K1, YO, K11] 4 times.

Round 31 (Dec): [K2tog, K6, K2tog, YO, K3, YO, K1, Sl1, K1, psso, K3, K2tog, K1, YO, K3, YO, Sl1, K1, psso, K5, Sl1, K1, psso] 4 times, 128 sts.

Round 32: [K9, YO, Sl1, K1, psso, K2, YO, K1, Sl1, K1, psso, K1, K2tog, K1, YO, K2, K2tog, YO, K8] 4 times.

Round 33 (Dec): [K2tog, K8, YO, Sl1, K1, psso, K2, YO, K1, Sl1, K2tog, psso, K1, YO, K2, K2tog, YO, K7, Sl1, K1, psso] 4 times, 120 sts.

Round 34: [K14, YO, Sl1, K2tog, psso, K13] 4 times.

Round 35 (Dec): [K2tog, K11, K2tog, YO, K1, YO, Sl1, K1, psso, K10, Sl1, K1, psso] 4 times, 112 sts.

Round 36: [K11, K2tog, YO, K3, YO, Sl1, K1, psso, K10] 4 times.

Round 37 (Dec): [K2tog, K8, K2tog, YO, K5, YO, Sl1, K1, psso, K7, Sl1, K1, psso] 4 times, 104 sts.

Round 38: [K10, YO, Sl1, K1, psso, K3, K2tog, YO, K9] 4 times.

Round 39 (Dec): [K2tog, K9, YO, Sl1, K1, psso, K1, K2tog, YO, K8, Sl1, K1, psso] 4 times, 96 sts.

Round 40: [K11, YO, Sl1, K2tog, psso, YO, K10] 4 times.

K each following round AND AT THE SAME TIME continue to dec 8 sts on next and 5 foll alt rounds as before, 48 sts. K one round.

Next round: K2tog to end of round, 24 sts.
Break yarn leaving a long end, draw yarn through rem sts and draw together firmly. Finish off securely and darn in all ends.

MAKING UP

Dampen beret and place on a small dinner plate, gently steaming work with a hot iron then leaving to dry.

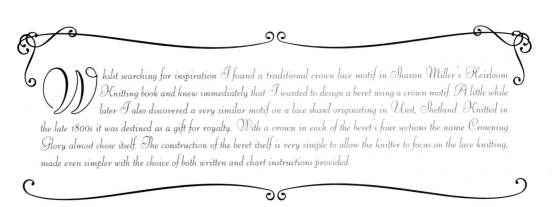

Whilst searching for inspiration I found a traditional crown lace motif in Sharon Miller's Heirloom Knitting book and knew immediately that I wanted to design a beret using a crown motif. A little while later I also discovered a very similar motif on a lace shawl originating in Unst, Shetland. Knitted in the late 1800s it was destined as a gift for royalty. With a crown in each of the beret's four sections the name Crowning Glory almost chose itself. The construction of the beret itself is very simple to allow the knitter to focus on the lace knitting, made even simpler with the choice of both written and chart instructions provided.

Diamond Stole

MATERIALS

Juno Belle, 70% UK Alpaca / 30% Bluefaced Leicester
(400m / 437yds per 100g skein)
(lightweight 4 ply / fingering weight)
2 skeins shade Heart on my Sleeve – 124g used to
complete stole to length specified. There is enough
remaining to make the stole longer if required.
1 pair 3.5mm (US #4) needles
Stitch marker
A small quantity of 4ply waste yarn

TENSION

21 st repeat = 8½cm (3¼in) and 48 row repeat = 14½cm
(5¾in) (after blocking) using 3.5mm needles. See guidance
below for working tension square

ABBREVIATIONS

See page 95

SIZING

Finished Length (after blocking) 148cm (58½in)
Finished Width (after blocking) 31cm (12in)

PATTERN NOTES

To work tension square cast on 34 sts using 3.5mm
needles. If working from chart work from right to
left across 34 sts as shown on row 1 of chart. If
working from written instructions work as set
below, working section marked with * once only.
Continue in pattern until all 48 rows have been
completed. Cast off fairly loosely. Wash swatch and
block. Total width of swatch should equal 14cm
(5½in) and total length should equal 14½cm
(5¾in).

The stole commences with a provisional cast on
using waste yarn, followed by a garter stitch edging
then the 48 row pattern repeat, worked 9 times in
total with rows 1–24 repeated once more. A garter
stitch edging is then worked before commencing the
top lace edge. Once this is completed the bottom
lace edge is worked downwards from the provisional
cast on.

STOLE

Using 3.5mm needles and waste yarn, cast on 78
sts, place a marker at the end of this row. Change to
main yarn and work as folls:

Next row: Sl1 pwise wyif, K2tog, K to last 3 sts,
K2tog, K1, 76 sts.

Next row (RS): Sl1 pwise wyif, K to end.
Rep this row twice more.

Now work in main patt as follows: (also shown on
chart)

Row 1 (RS): Sl1 pwise wyif, K2, * K1, YO, Sl1, K1,
psso, K1, K2tog, YO, K2, YO, Sl1, K1, psso, K2,
YO, K2tog, Sl1, K1, psso, YO, K2, K2tog, YO, K1,
rep from * to last 10 sts, K1, YO, Sl1, K1, psso, K1,
K2tog, YO, K4.

Row 2: Sl1 pwise wyif, K2, P to last 3 sts, K3.

Row 3: Sl1 pwise wyif, K2, * YO, Sl1, K1, psso,
YO, Sl1, K2tog, psso, YO, K2tog, YO, Sl1, K1,
psso, YO, Sl1, K1, psso, K1, YO, K2tog, Sl1, K1,
psso, YO, K1, K2tog, YO, K2tog, rep from * to last

Chart

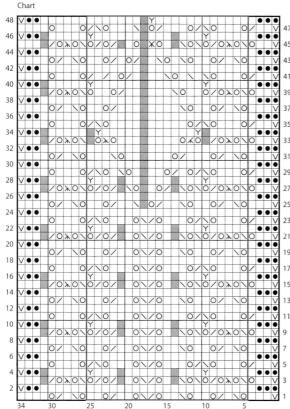

Key

- ☐ Knit on RS, Purl on WS
- ● Purl on RS, Knit on WS
- ◣ Sl1, K1, psso
- ◢ K2tog
- ◤ Sl1, K2tog, psso
- O Yarnover
- ▨ No stitch, ignore these squares and move straight to next knitting instruction
- V Sl1 pwise wyif
- Y Wfb – work into front and back of stitch (see abbreviations)
- ◸ K3tog
- ✕ 2 stitches from 3 (see abbreviations)
- ☐ Pattern repeat

K1, psso, K2tog, YO, K2tog, rep from * to last 10 sts, YO, Sl1, K1, psso, YO, Sl1, K2tog, psso, YO, K2tog, K3, 66 sts.

Row 28: Sl1 pwise wyif, K2, * P5, Wfb, P11, Wfb, rep from * to last 9 sts, P6, K3, 72 sts.

Row 29: Sl1 pwise wyif, K2, * K2tog, YO, K3, YO, Sl1, K1, psso, K2tog, YO, K1, K2tog, YO, K3, YO, Sl1, K1, psso, K1, YO, Sl1, K1, psso, rep from * to last 9 sts, K2tog, YO, K3, YO, K4, 73 sts.

Row 30: Sl1 pwise wyif, K2, P to last 3 sts, K3.

Row 31: Sl1 pwise wyif, K2, * K1, YO, Sl1, K1, psso, K1, K2tog, YO, K3, YO, K5, YO, Sl1, K1, psso, K2, rep from * to last 10 sts, K1, YO, Sl1, K1, psso, K1, K2tog, YO, K4.

Row 32: Sl1 pwise wyif, K2, P to last 3 sts, K3.

Row 33: Sl1 pwise wyif, K2, * YO, Sl1, K1, psso, YO, Sl1, K2tog, psso, YO, K2tog, YO, K3tog, YO, K7, YO, Sl1, K2tog, psso, rep from * to last 10 sts, YO, Sl1, K1, psso, YO, Sl1, K2tog, psso, YO, K2tog, K3, 66 sts.

Row 34: Sl1 pwise wyif, K2, * P5, Wfb, P11, Wfb, rep from * to last 9 sts, P6, K3, 72 sts.

Row 35: Sl1 pwise wyif, K2, * K2tog, YO, K3, YO, Sl1, K1, psso, K2tog, YO, K9, YO, Sl1, K1, psso, rep from * to last 9 sts, K2tog, YO, K3, YO, K4, 73 sts.

Row 36: Sl1 pwise wyif, K2, P to last 3 sts, K3.

Row 37: Sl1 pwise wyif, K2, * K1, YO, Sl1, K1, psso, K1, K2tog, YO, K2, YO, Sl1, K1, psso, K7, K2tog, YO, K1, rep from * to last 10 sts, K1, YO, Sl1, K1, psso, K1, K2tog, YO, K4.

Row 38: Sl1 pwise wyif, K2, P to last 3 sts, K3.

10 sts, YO, Sl1, K1, psso, YO, Sl1, K2tog, psso, YO, K2tog, K3, 69 sts.

Row 4: Sl1 pwise wyif, K2, * P5, Wfb, P12, Wfb, rep from * to last 9 sts, P6, K3, 75 sts.

Row 5: Sl1 pwise wyif, K2, * K2tog, YO, K3, YO, Sl1, K1, psso, K2tog, YO, K3, YO, K2tog, Sl1, K1, psso, YO, K3, YO, Sl1, K1, psso, rep from * to last 9 sts, K2tog, YO, K3, YO, K4, 76 sts.

Row 6: Sl1 pwise wyif, K2, P to last 3 sts, K3.

Rep these 6 rows 3 times more (24 rows worked in total).

Row 25: Sl1 pwise wyif, K2, * K1, YO, Sl1, K1, psso, K1, K2tog, YO, K2, YO, Sl1, K1, psso, K2, K2tog, YO, Sl1, K1, psso, K2, K2tog, YO, K1, rep from * to last 10 sts, K1, YO, Sl1, K1, psso, K1, K2tog, YO, K4, 73 sts.

Row 26: Sl1 pwise wyif, K2, P to last 3 sts, K3.

Row 27: Sl1 pwise wyif, K2, * YO, Sl1, K1, psso, YO, Sl1, K2tog, psso, YO, K2tog, YO, Sl1, K1, psso, YO, Sl1, K1, psso, K2tog, YO, K1, YO, Sl1,

Row 39: Sl1 pwise wyif, K2, * YO, Sl1, K1, psso, YO, Sl1, K2tog, psso, YO, K2tog, YO, K2, YO, Sl1, K1, psso, K5, K2tog, YO, K2, rep from * to last 10 sts, YO, Sl1, K1, psso, YO, Sl1, K2tog, psso, YO, K2tog, K3, 72 sts.

Row 40: Sl1 pwise wyif, K2, * P5, Wfb, P13, Wfb, rep from * to last 9 sts P6, K3, 78 sts.

Row 41: Sl1 pwise wyif, K2, * K2tog, YO, K3, YO, [Sl1, K1, psso, K1] twice, YO, Sl1, K1, psso, K3, K2tog, YO, K1, K2tog, K1, rep from * to last 9 sts, K2tog, YO, K3, YO, K4, 73 sts.

Row 42: Sl1 pwise wyif, K2, P to last 3 sts, K3.

Row 43: Sl1 pwise wyif, K2, * K1, YO, Sl1, K1, psso, K1, K2tog, YO, K2, YO, Sl1, K1, psso, K1, YO, Sl1, K1, psso, [K1, K2tog, YO] twice, K1, rep from * to last 10 sts, K1, YO, Sl1, K1, psso, K1, K2tog, YO, K4.

Row 44: Sl1 pwise wyif, K2, P to last 3 sts, K3.

Row 45: Sl1 pwise wyif, K2, * YO, Sl1, K1, psso, YO, Sl1, K2tog, psso, YO, K2tog, YO, Sl1, K1, psso, YO, Sl1, K1, psso, K1, YO, 2 stitches from 3, YO, K1, K2tog, YO, K2tog, rep from * to last 10 sts, YO, Sl1, K1, psso, YO, Sl1, K2tog, psso, YO, K2tog, K3, 69 sts.

Row 46: Sl1 pwise wyif, K2, * P5, Wfb, P12, Wfb, rep from * to last 9 sts, P6, K3, 75 sts.

Row 47: Sl1 pwise wyif, K2, * K2tog, YO, K3, YO, Sl1, K1, psso, K2tog, YO, K3, K2tog, YO, Sl1, K1, psso, K3, YO, Sl1, K1, psso, rep from * to last 9 sts, K2tog, YO, K3, YO, K4, 73 sts.

Row 48: Sl1 pwise wyif, K2, P13, Wfb, * P19, Wfb, rep from * to last 16 sts, P13, K3, 76 sts.

Rep these 48 rows a further 8 times, then work rows 1–24 once more.

Next row: Sl1 pwise wyif, K to end.
Rep this row twice more.
Next row: Sl1 pwise wyif, K37, Kfb, K to end, 77 sts.

Lace Edging

Next row (RS): Sl1 pwise wyif, K2, * K1, YO, K3,
Sl1, K2tog, psso, K3, YO, rep from * to last 4 sts, K4.
Next row: Sl1 pwise wyif, K2, P to last 3 sts, K3.
Rep these 2 rows a further 6 times (14 rows worked
in total) then rep first row once more.
Next row (WS): Sl1 pwise wyif, K to end.
Next row (RS): Sl1 pwise wyif, K to end.
Cast off.

Returning to cast on edge and commencing at
marked end, carefully remove waste yarn, and place
the 77 live sts onto 3.5mm needle. When removing
the provisional cast on you will have one less whole
st than you initially cast on. Ensure the RS of the
work is facing you on completion. You will now be
working downwards from the remainder of the
work.

Lace Edging

Next row (RS): Sl1 pwise wyif, K2, * K1, YO, K3,
Sl1, K2tog, psso, K3, YO, rep from * to last 4 sts, K4.
Next row: Sl1 pwise wyif, K2, P to last 3 sts, K3.
Rep these 2 rows a further 6 times (14 rows worked
in total) then rep first row once more.
Next row (WS): Sl1 pwise wyif, K to end.
Next row (RS): Sl1 pwise wyif, K to end.
Cast off.

MAKING UP

Handwash stole and squeeze dry. Pin scarf out to
required measurements, pinning the (YO, K1, YO)
sts of the lace edging into points as shown. When
stole is dry remove pins and darn in all ends
carefully.

Looking through an early 1950s needlecraft book I found the basis of this beautiful diamond pattern in a design for a table mat and instantly realised it was far too good to be covered with a dinner plate. The pattern includes small diamonds, half diamonds and a large central diamond in each pattern repeat so couldn't be more appropriate. The pattern looks very different depending on whether it is viewed draped vertically or horizontally across the shoulders. Once the pattern is placed it is surprisingly easy to knit but the use of stitch markers and life lines would make it even easier for the novice lace knitter. The stole is designed to be just under 5 feet in length but there is enough yarn remaining from the second skein to make the stole significantly longer if preferred.

Lion and Unicorn

MATERIALS

Excelana Luxury 4 Ply Wool 100% pure new British wool (159m / 174yds per 50g ball)
6 (7, 8, 8, 9, 9, 10, 10, 11, 12) balls
shade Cornflower Blue – MC
1 ball shade Alabaster – CC
1 pair 2.75mm (US #2) needles
1 pair 3mm (US #2–3) needles
1 set of 3mm (US #2–3) double pointed needles (DPNs)
or 40cm long 3mm (US #2–3) circular needle

Small quantities of red and gold embroidery threads for Swiss darning and embroidery (Optional)

TENSION

28 sts & 36 rows = 10cm (4in) using 3mm needles over stocking stitch

ABBREVIATIONS

See page 95

SIZING

To Fit	cm	81	86	92	97	102	107	112	117	122	127
	(in)	(32)	(34)	(36)	(38)	(40)	(42)	(44)	(46)	(48)	(50)
Actual Bust Size	cm	87	93	98½	103	108½	113	118½	123	128½	133
	(in)	(34¼)	(36½)	(38¾)	(40½)	(42¾)	(44½)	(46¾)	(48¼)	(50½)	(52¼)
Length to Underarm	cm	25	26	27	27	28	28	29	30	31	32
	(in)	(9¾)	(10¼)	(10¾)	(10¾)	(11)	(11)	(11¼)	(11¾)	(12¼)	(12¾)
Armhole Depth	cm	27½	28½	29	30½	31	31½	32	33	33	34
	(in)	(10¾)	(11¼)	(11½)	(12)	(12¼)	(12¼)	(12½)	(13)	(13)	(13½)
Finished Length	cm	52½	54½	56½	57½	58½	59	61	63	64	66½
	(in)	(20¾)	(21½)	(22¼)	(22¾)	(23)	(23¼)	(24)	(24¾)	(25¼)	(26¼)
Sleeve Length	cm	33	33	34	34	35½	35½	35½	36½	36½	36½
	(in)	(13)	(13)	(13½)	(13½)	(14)	(14)	(14)	(14½)	(14½)	(14½)
Back Neck Width	cm	13	15	15	15	16½	16½	16½	18	18	18
	(in)	(5)	(6)	(6)	(6)	(6½)	(6½)	(6½)	(7)	(7)	(7)

Model is shown wearing size to fit chest 81cm (32in)

PATTERN NOTES

This garment is knitted in one piece from lower cast on edge of front, incorporating the Lion and the Unicorn motif worked using combination intarsia technique. Use separate small balls of CC for each main area of both the Lion and the Unicorn so that CC is not carried across large areas of MC. For example, each leg should use a separate ball of CC. Additionally separate balls of MC should be used between these sections of CC. Where only a single st is worked in CC it is better to carry MC across the back of this st rather than using two separate balls. The garment continues in one piece with increases being worked at each side to create sleeves. Once the shoulder line is worked using short row shaping, the back of the garment is then worked from the top down, decreasing stitches to work the 'back' of the sleeves.

FRONT
(worked from bottom up)

Using 2.75mm needles and MC, cast on 98 (106, 114, 120, 128, 134, 142, 148, 156, 162) sts.
Row 1 (RS): * K1, P1, rep from * to end.
Rep this row a further three times, then join in CC, and rep this row twice more. Change back to MC and continue to work in rib as set until work measures 10cm (4in) ending with a WS row. Change to 3mm needles and commencing with a K row, work in stocking stitch for 6 (10, 14, 14, 16, 16, 8, 10, 14, 14) rows.

Shape Sides
Next row (RS): K1, M1, K to last st, M1, K1, 100 (108, 116, 122, 130, 136, 144, 150, 158, 164) sts.
Work 3 rows in stocking stitch.
Rep last 4 rows a further 11 (11, 11, 11, 11, 11, 5, 4, 4, 2) times, 122 (130, 138, 144, 152, 158, 154, 158, 166, 168) sts.

7th, 8th, 9th and 10th sizes only
Next row (RS): K1, M1, K to last st, M1, K1.
Work 5 rows in stocking stitch. Rep last 6 rows 5 (6, 6, 8) more times, (166, 172, 180, 186) sts.

Shape Sleeves (all sizes)
Next row (RS): Cast on 69 (69, 72, 72, 75, 75, 75, 79, 79, 79) sts, K to end of row, 191 (199, 210, 216, 227, 233, 241, 251, 259, 265) sts.

Next row: Cast on 69 (69, 72, 72, 75, 75, 75, 79, 79, 79) sts, P to end of row 260 (268, 282, 288, 302, 308, 316, 330, 338, 344) sts.
Continue shaping by inc 1 st at each end of next row, then every foll 6th (6th, 6th, 6th, 6th, 7th, 7th, 7th, 8th, 8th) row, 3 times (4 times in total), 268 (276, 290, 296, 310, 316, 324, 338, 346, 352) sts.
Work 3 (3, 3, 3, 3, 4, 4, 4, 5, 5) rows without shaping.

** Place Chart (Please read pattern notes on working from chart)

Next row (RS): K97 (101, 108, 111, 118, 121, 125, 132, 136, 139) in MC, reading from right to left, work row 1 of chart, K97 (101, 108, 111, 118, 121, 125, 132, 136, 139) in MC.
Next row: P97 (101, 108, 111, 118, 121, 125, 132, 136, 139) in MC, reading from left to right, work row 2 of chart, P97 (101, 108, 111, 118, 121, 125, 132, 136, 139) in MC.
Continue to work 74 sts of chart and st st either side as set until chart row 21 (21, 21, 21, 21, 24, 24, 24, 27, 27) is complete, and AT SAME TIME continue to shape sleeves by inc 1 st at each end of next and every foll 6th (6th, 6th, 6th, 6th, 7th, 7th, 7th, 8th, 8th) row until 276 (284, 298, 304, 318, 324, 332, 346, 354, 360) sts.
Now continue to work from chart as set for 3 (7, 7, 11, 13, 8, 10, 14, 7, 11) rows without further shaping.

Chart

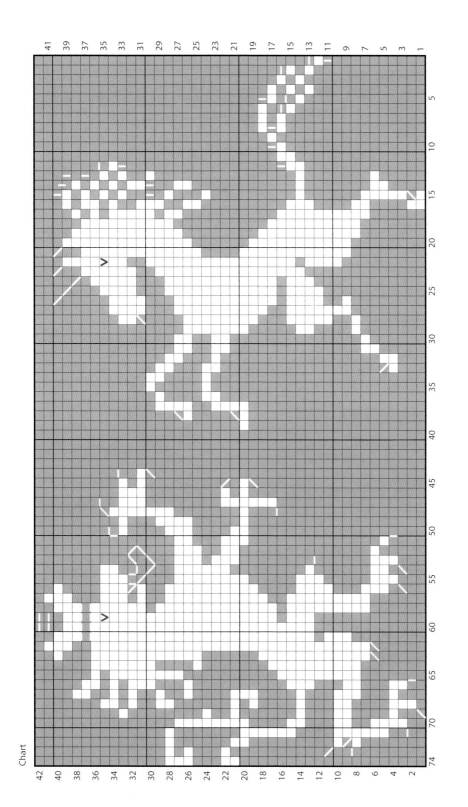

Key

☐ White; Knit on RS, Purl on WS

▨ Blue; Knit on RS, Purl on WS

❯ White; Knit on RS, Purl on WS; Swiss Darn in Red after knitting

▧ Blue; Knit on RS, Purl on WS; Gold embroidery applied after knitting (Optional)

Shape Shoulders

Keeping chart correct as set until all 42 rows are complete, then working in MC only, work short row shaping as foll:

Next row (RS): K to last 5 (5, 5, 5, 5, 5, 5, 6, 6, 6) sts, w&t.

Next row (WS): P to last 5 (5, 5, 5, 5, 5, 5, 6, 6, 6) sts, w&t.

Next row: K to last 10 (10, 10, 10, 10, 10, 10, 12, 12, 12) sts, w&t.

Next row: P to last 10 (10, 10, 10, 10, 10, 10, 12, 12, 12) sts, w&t.

Next row: K to last 15 (15, 15, 15, 15, 15, 15, 18, 18, 18) sts, w&t.

Next row: P to last 15 (15, 15, 15, 15, 15, 15, 18, 18, 18) sts, w&t.

Continue as set working 5 (5, 5, 5, 5, 5, 5, 6, 6, 6) less sts on each subsequent pair of rows until 20 (20, 20, 20, 20, 20, 20, 20, 18) short rows have been worked in total (50, 50, 50, 50, 50, 50, 50, 60, 60, 54) sts unworked at each end.

Shape Neck

Next row (RS): K78 (79, 86, 89, 94, 97, 101, 96, 100, 109), K2tog, turn, leaving rem 146 (153, 160, 163, 172, 175, 179, 188, 192, 195) sts on spare needle or holder.

Next row: P to last 55 (55, 55, 55, 55, 55, 55, 66, 66, 60) sts, w&t.

Continue in this manner, working 5 (5, 5, 5, 5, 5, 5, 6, 6, 6) sts less on each WS row and K2tog at neck edge of next and 8 foll RS rows. Now keeping neck edge straight continue working short row shaping as set until only 5 (6, 8, 11, 16, 19, 23, 4, 8, 11) sts are worked.

Next row (WS): P across all left arm and shoulder sts, picking up wraps & working together with sts along row, 120 (121, 128, 131, 136, 139, 143, 148, 152, 155) sts.

Next row (RS): K.

Next row (WS): Cast on 5 sts, P to end, 125 (126, 133, 136, 141, 144, 148, 153, 157, 160) sts.

Next row: K.

Next row: Cast on 5 sts, P to end, 130 (131, 138, 141, 146, 149, 153, 158, 162, 165) sts. Place these sts on a spare needle.

Return to remaining 146 (153, 160, 163, 172, 175, 179, 188, 192, 195) sts, and place centre 16 (22, 22, 22, 26, 26, 26, 30, 30, 30) sts on a holder. With RS facing, rejoin MC to rem sts at neck edge and K to last 55 (55, 55, 55, 55, 55, 55, 66, 66, 60) sts, w&t.

Next row (WS): P to last 2 sts, P2togtbl.

Continue in this manner, working 5 (5, 5, 5, 5, 5, 5, 6, 6, 6) sts less on each RS row and P2togtbl at neck edge of next and 8 foll WS rows. Now keeping neck edge straight continue working short row shaping as set until only 5 (6, 8, 11, 16, 19, 23, 4, 8, 11) sts are worked.

Next row (RS): K across all right arm and shoulder sts, picking up wraps & working together with sts along row (120, 121, 128, 131, 136, 139, 143, 148, 152, 155 sts).

Next row (WS): P.

Next row (RS): Cast on 5 sts, K to end (125, 126, 133, 136, 141, 144, 148, 153, 157, 160 sts).

Next row: P.

Next row: Cast on 5 sts, K to end (130, 131, 138, 141, 146, 149, 153, 158, 162, 165 sts).

Joining row

P across all 130 (131, 138, 141, 146, 149, 153, 158, 162, 165) sts on needle, cast on 16 (22, 22, 22, 26, 26, 26, 30, 30, 30) sts, then P across all 130 (131, 138, 141, 146, 149, 153, 158, 162, 165) sts held on spare needle for left side, 276 (284, 298, 304, 318, 324, 332, 346, 354, 360) sts.

Shape Shoulders

Next row (RS): K161 (169, 178, 184, 198, 204, 212, 202, 210, 216) sts, w&t.

Next row (WS): P46 (54, 58, 64, 78, 84, 92, 58, 66, 72) sts, w&t.

Next row (RS): K51 (59, 63, 69, 83, 89, 97, 64, 72, 78) sts, w&t.

Next row (WS): P56 (64, 68, 74, 88, 94, 102, 70, 78, 84) sts, w&t.

Continue in this manner, working an additional 5 (5, 5, 5, 5, 5, 5, 6, 6, 6) sts on each row until all 276 (284, 298, 304, 318, 324, 332, 346, 354, 360) sts have been worked, picking up wraps and working them with sts as you reach them.

Shape Cuff

Now working in stocking stitch, work 3 (7, 7, 11, 13, 8, 10, 14, 7, 11) rows straight, then dec 1 st at each end of next and every foll 6th (6th, 6th, 6th, 7th, 7th, 7th, 8th, 8th) row until 260 (268, 282, 288, 302, 308, 316, 330, 338, 344) sts.

Next row (RS): Cast off 69 (69, 72, 72, 75, 75, 75, 79, 79, 79) sts, patt to end, 191 (199, 210, 216, 227, 233, 241, 251, 259, 265) sts.

Next row (WS): Cast off 69 (69, 72, 72, 75, 75, 75, 79, 79, 79) sts, patt to end 122 (130, 138, 144, 152, 158, 166, 172, 180, 186) sts.

Shape Sides

Knit 1 row.

7th, 8th, 9th and 10th sizes only

Work 5 rows in stocking stitch, then dec 1 st at each end of next row.

Rep last 6 rows 5 (6, 6, 8) more times, (154, 158, 166, 168) sts.

All sizes

Work 3 rows in stocking stitch, then dec 1 st at each end of next row.

Rep last 4 rows a further 11 (11, 11, 11, 11, 11, 5, 4, 4, 2) times, 98 (106, 114, 120, 128, 134, 142, 148, 156, 162) sts.

Work straight for 5 (9, 13, 13, 15, 15, 7, 9, 13, 13) rows, ending with a WS row.

Change to 2.75mm needles and work in rib for 10cm (4in) as set for front.

Cast off fairly loosely in rib.

MAKING UP

Darn in all ends working ends around edges of motifs rather than across. Press work on WS of work through a damp cloth.

NECKBAND

Using 3mm dpn's or circular needle and MC, and with RS facing, commence at back neck and pick up and K 36 (42, 42, 42, 46, 46, 46, 50, 50, 50) sts across back neck, then pick up and K 26 (26, 28, 28, 28, 28, 28, 28, 28, 30) sts down left side neck, then K across 16 (22, 22, 22, 26, 26, 26, 30, 30, 30) sts on holder at centre front neck, then pick up and K 26 (26, 28, 28, 28, 28, 28, 28, 28, 30) sts up right side neck, 104 (116, 120, 120, 128, 128, 128, 136, 136, 140) sts. PM at end of round.

Next Round: * K1, P1, rep from * to end. Rep this round a further 4 times, then change to CC and work 2 rounds in rib. Change back to MC and work 1 round in rib, then cast off loosely in rib. (Use larger needle for cast off row if necessary).

CUFFS

Using 2.75mm needles and MC, and with RS facing, pick and K 72 (72, 72, 72, 72, 84, 84, 84, 96, 96) sts along sleeve cuff edge.

Next row (RS): * K1, P1, rep from * to end. Rep this row 23 times more, then join in CC and work 2 rows in rib, Change back to MC and work 4 rows in rib, then cast off in rib.

Sew up side seams and darn in any remaining ends.

Using red embroidery thread Swiss darn over a single stitch for eye as shown on chart for both the Lion and the Unicorn. Using gold embroidery thread work running stitch as shown on chart for claws, unicorn horn etc., if required.

27½ (28½, 29, 30½, 31, 31½, 32, 33, 33, 34) cm

52½ (54½, 56½, 57½, 58½, 59, 61, 63, 64, 66½) cm

43½ (46½, 49, 51½, 54, 56½, 59, 61½, 64, 66½) cm

24½ (24½, 25½, 24½, 27, 27, 27, 28, 28, 28) cm

25 (26, 27, 27, 28, 28, 29, 30, 31, 32) cm

The original of this pattern can be found in the 'Coronation' issue of Stitchcraft in 1953. However the front and back were knitted in two separate pieces which resulted in a seam running the length of each shoulder and down the top of each arm (in addition to the underarm seam). The original pattern also had a much higher and tighter neck which most people today would find very restrictive to wear. In addition to this it was only a single sized pattern. However the bat-wing sleeves, such a popular design element of the 1950s, and the Lion and the Unicorn motifs were too good to pass by.

I therefore re-wrote the pattern for the garment to be knitted in one piece, beginning at the bottom front, then short rows worked to create the shoulder and arm shaping on both the front and the back and then down the other side for the back. The introduction of a wide range of sizes means we can all have our own Lion and Unicorn jumper.

Retro Jubilee Socks

MATERIALS
Jamieson & Smith 2 Ply Jumper Weight 100% Shetland wool (115m / 125yds per 25g ball)
3 balls shade 202 – A
3 balls shade FC15 – B
2 balls shade 1403 – C
1 set of 2.75mm (US #2) double pointed needles (DPNs)
1 set of 3mm (US #2-3) double pointed needles (DPNs)
(or your preferred needles for working small diameters in the round)

Stitch markers

TENSION
36 sts & 40 rows = 10cm (4in) using 3mm needles over chequer stitch pattern.

ABBREVIATIONS
See page 95

SIZING

To Fit		Women's UK size 7 [US 9½, Euro 40]	Men's UK size 11 [US 11½, Euro 45]
Sock Circumference	cm	20	24½
	(in)	(7¾)	(9½)
Sock Leg Length	cm	10	20
to top of heel	(in)	(4)	(7¾)
Sock Foot Length	cm	24	28
including toe	(in)	(9½)	(11)
shaping of 7cm (2¾in)			

To alter length of foot simply adjust rounds worked after heel completed and before toe commences.
To alter length of leg adjust number of rounds worked before commencing heel shaping, taking care to finish with round 6 of pattern.

PATTERN NOTES
These socks are knitted in the round from the top down. This pattern uses a particular shaping method at the turning of the heel to prevent holes appearing when short rows are worked. This involves working a **slyo** (slipped yarnover) as follows:

After turning work at directed point, bring yarn to the front as though to purl. With right needle, slip the next stitch purlwise. Take the yarn over the top of the right hand needle to the back of the work, pulling tightly so that both 'legs' of the stitch below are stretched over the needle.

If on a RS row yarn is already in correct position to K the next st.
If on a WS row now bring yarn to the front of work before working the next st.

After working a slyo it will be necessary on a subsequent row to work the slyo. To do so, insert the right needle under BOTH legs of the st that have been stretched over the needle and then either K or P together depending on what side of work you are on. It is important that the slyo is not mistaken for two separate stitches as this would result in an increased st if they are worked separately.

CHEQUER STITCH PATTERN

(rep of 4 sts and 6 rounds, also shown on chart)

Round 1: K1A, * K2B, K2A, rep from * to last 3 sts, K2B, K1A.

Round 2: As round 1.

Round 3: K1C, * K2A, K2C, rep from * to last 3 sts, K2A, K1C.

Round 4: As round 3.

Round 5: K1B, * K2C, K2B, rep from * to last 3 sts, K2C, K1B.

Round 6: As round 5.

These 6 rounds form pattern.

CUFF

Using 2.75mm double pointed needles and B, cast on 80 (88) sts. Distribute sts evenly over your needles. Join work into a round taking care not to twist stitches, placing stitch marker at join (this marks centre back) and commence working as folls:

Round 1 (RS): Using A, * K1, P1, rep from * to end. Rep this round until work measures 5cm (2in).

LEG

Commencing with round 1 and using 3mm dpns work chequer stitch pattern from either chart or written instructions, until work measures 10 (20) cm (4, 7¾ in) or required length, ending with a round 6.

HEEL

Break off yarns A and C. Heel is worked back and forth in yarn B only.

HEEL TOP

Shape heel using short rows as folls:

Row 1 (RS): Using B K20 (22), turn, leaving next 40 (44) sts on a spare needle for top of foot.

Row 2: Slyo, P39 (43), turn.

Row 3: Slyo, K to slyo created on prev row, turn.

Row 4: Slyo, P to slyo created on prev row, turn.

Rep last 2 rows 11 more times, then work row 3 once more but do not turn. There will now be 13 slyo sts at each end of the heel and 14 (18) plain stitches at centre.

It is now necessary to work in the round across all sts before returning to work short rows again for heel base. Break off yarn B and with RS facing rejoin at beg of heel sts on needle.

Round 1 (RS): K across all heel sts in B taking care to knit each slyo st as 1 st, join in A and matching patt, work from round 1 of chart or written

instructions across next 40 (44) sts, break off A.

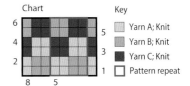

Chart

Key
Yarn A; Knit
Yarn B; Knit
Yarn C; Knit
Pattern repeat

Round 2: K across all heels sts using B, join in A and again matching patt, work from round 2 of chart across next 40 (44) sts, break off A.

HEEL BASE

Using B, work short rows again back and forth across 40 (44) heel sts only as folls:

Row 1 (RS): K to last 12 sts, turn.

Row 2: Slyo, P15 (19), turn.

Row 3: Slyo, K to slyo created on prev row, knit slyo as 1 st, K1, turn.

Row 4: Slyo, P to slyo created on prev row, purl slyo as 1 st, P1, turn.

Rep last 2 rows 11 more times.

Next row: Slyo, K to beg of round marker. Remove marker then with another needle K to slyo created on prev row, knit slyo as 1 st, PM for new beg of round.

FOOT

The top of foot and sole of sock are now worked together in the round as folls:

Next round: Join in yarns A and C and matching patt, work round 3 from chart or written instructions, then continue in chequer patt across all sts of sole, remembering to knit rem slyo as 1 st, 80 (88) sts. Continue working in patt across all sts until foot measures 17 (21) cm (6½, 8¼in) from back of heel (or 7cm (2¾in) less than desired foot length) ending with a row 2 or 6 of chequer pattern.

TOE

Using B only work as folls:

Round 1: * K1, SSK, K34 (38), K2tog, K1, PM, rep from * once more, 76 (84) sts.

Round 2: K.

Round 3: * K1, SSK, K to 3 sts before marker, K2tog, K1, SM, rep from * once more, 72 (80) sts.

Round 4: K.

Rep last 2 rounds 11 more times, 28 (36) sts. Arrange first 14 (18) sts on one needle and second 14 (18) sts on second needle and cut yarn leaving a 25cm (10in) tail. Graft these sts together. Darn in all ends. Block.

rowing through another early 1950s needlecraft book, I found this great chequer pattern being used as a cardigan trim. I have something of a penchant for multi-coloured socks and decided that this would be the perfect pattern to use for my unisex retro jubilee socks. An auto heel is worked in one colour and then the multi coloured pattern continues down the sock to the toe which is again worked in only one colour. The leg of the sock can be worked as long or as short as you prefer, depending on how much yarn you have at your disposal and personal preference. Keep the toes and heel in the same colour or go for the toes in blue and the heels in red or even one of each!

Amies

MATERIALS
JC Rennie 4 ply Lambswool 100% wool
(246m / 270yds per 50g ball)
– or –
Albayarn 4 ply Lambswool 100% wool, (225m per 50g ball)
4 (4, 5, 7, 8) balls, shade 200 (Winter White)
1 pair 3.25mm (US #3) needles
1 3.25mm (US #3) (40cm) circular needle
Stitch holders

TENSION
To work tension square cast on 35 sts and work 3 patt reps.

Cast off sample, dampen and pin out on towel or blanket,
leave to dry, then measure.
1 patt repeat = 4cm (1½in) in width using 3.25mm
needles when blocked
1 patt repeat = 5cm (2in) in height using 3.25mm needles
when blocked
– or –
27½ sts & 36 rows = 10cm (4in) using 3.25mm needles
over pattern when blocked

ABBREVIATIONS
See page 95

SIZING

		Petite	Standard			
To Fit	cm	76–81	76–81	92–97	107–112	122–127
	(in)	(30–32)	(30–32)	(36–38)	(42–44)	(48–50)
Actual Bust Size	cm	73½	73½	89½	105½	121½
	(in)	(29)	(29)	(35¼)	(41½)	(47¾)
Length to Underarm	cm	30	33½	37	40	43½
	(in)	(11¾)	(13)	(14¾)	(15¾)	(17)
Armhole Depth	cm	18	19½	21½	23	25
	(in)	(7)	(7¾)	(8½)	(9)	(9¾)
Finished Length	cm	48	53	59	63	68½
	(in)	(18¾)	(20¾)	(23¼)	(24¾)	(27)
Sleeve Length	cm	15	15	15	17	17
	(in)	(6)	(6)	(6)	(6¾)	(6¾)
Shoulder to Shoulder	cm	32½	32½	35½	38	41
	(in)	(12¾)	(12¾)	(14)	(15)	(16¼)
Back Neck Width	cm	12½	12½	15½	16½	17
	(in)	(5)	(5)	(6¼)	(6½)	(6¾)

Worn with approx 3–7cm (1–3in) negative ease all round
Model is shown wearing size to fit chest 92–97cm (36–38in)

WORKING SHAPING IN LACE PATTERN
Where possible, shaping has been placed on WS
rows, so that it doesn't interfere with the lace
pattern. When maintaining pattern after shaping, be
sure to only work a lace increase (or decrease) if
there are sufficient sts for its matched decrease
(or increase). If in doubt, replace partial lace repeats
with stocking stitch at the sides.

STITCH PATTERN

(Patt rep = 11 sts + 2)

The following stitch pattern is also shown on the chart.

Row 1 (RS): K1, (K2togtbl, K3, YO, K1, YO, K3, K2tog), K1.

Row 2 and all foll alt rows: P.

Row 3: As row 1.

Row 5: K1, (K2togtbl, K2, YO, K3, YO, K2, K2tog), K1.

Row 7: K1, (K2togtbl, K1, YO, K2togtbl, YO, K1, YO, K2tog, YO, K1, K2tog), K1.

Row 9: K1, (K2togtbl, YO, K2togtbl, [K1, YO] twice, K1, K2tog, YO, K2tog), K1.

Row 11: As row 9.

Row 13: K3, (YO, K3togtbl, YO, K1, YO, K3tog, YO, K4) to last 10 sts, YO, K3togtbl, YO, K1, YO, K3tog, YO, K3.

Row 15: K4, (YO, K1, K3tog, K1, YO, K6) to last 9 sts, YO, K1, K3tog, K1, YO, K4.

Row 17: K5, (YO, K3tog, YO, K8) to last 8 sts, YO, K3tog, YO, K5.

Row 18: P.

These 18 rows form pattern.

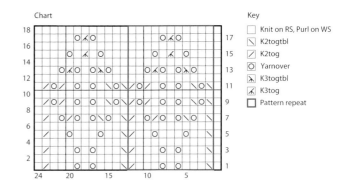

Chart

Key

- ☐ Knit on RS, Purl on WS
- ╲ K2togtbl
- ╱ K2tog
- ○ Yarnover
- ⋋ K3togtbl
- ⋌ K3tog
- ☐ Pattern repeat

BACK

Using 3.25mm needles, cast on 101 (101, 123, 145, 167) sts and commencing with row 1, work 18 rows of lace pattern. Rep these 18 rows a further 5 (5, 6, 7, 7) times.

2nd, 3rd and 5th sizes only

Work a further (12, 8, 12) rows in pattern.

All Sizes
Shape Armholes

Continuing to maintain pattern, cast off 3 (3, 3, 5, 6) sts at beg of next 2 (2, 4, 4, 4) rows, 95 (95, 111, 125, 143) sts, then dec 1 st at each end of next 3 (3,

6, 8, 10) rows, 89 (89, 99, 109, 123 sts).
Dec 1 st at each end of 0 (0, 1, 2, 7) foll
alt rows, 89 (89, 97, 105, 113) sts. ***

All Sizes

Work without further shaping until 64
(70, 78, 82, 90) rows worked from
commencement of armhole shaping. Last
row will be row 10 (10, 14, 10, 12) of
the 10th (11th, 12th, 13th, 14th) pattern
repeat.

Shape Shoulders

Continuing to maintain pattern, cast off
9 (9, 9, 10, 11) sts at beg of next 6 rows,
35 (35, 43, 45, 47) sts. Place rem sts on
holder.

FRONT

Work exactly as for back until ***.
Continuing to maintain pattern, work
without shaping until front measures 36
(36, 36, 38, 38) rows less than back to
start of shoulder shaping. Last row will
be row 10 (10, 14, 8, 10) of the 8th (9th,
10th, 11th, 12th) pattern repeat.

Divide for Neck

Next row (RS): Patt 36 (36, 39, 42, 45),
K2tog, turn, leaving rem 51 (51, 56, 61,
66) sts on holder.
Maintaining pattern, dec 1 st at neck
edge of next and 9 (9, 12, 12, 12) foll alt
rows, 27 (27, 27, 30, 33) sts rem.
Continue without further shaping until front
measures same as back to start of shoulder shaping,
(16 (16, 10, 12, 12) rows worked straight ending
with a WS row).

Shape Shoulder

Maintaining pattern, cast off 9 (9, 9, 10, 11) sts at
beg of next and 2 foll alt rows.

Leaving centre 13 (13, 15, 17, 19) sts on holder and
with RS facing, rejoin yarn to rem 38 (38, 41, 44,
47) sts.

Next row: K2tog, patt to end, 37 (37, 40, 43, 46 sts).
Dec 1 st at neck edge of next and 9 (9, 12, 12, 12)
foll alt rows, 27 (27, 27, 30, 33) sts.

Continuing to maintain pattern, work without
further shaping until front measures same as back to
start of shoulder shaping ending with a RS row (17
(17, 11, 13, 13) rows worked straight).

Shape Shoulder

Maintaining pattern, cast off 9 (9, 9, 10, 11) sts at
beg of next and 2 foll alt rows.

SLEEVES

Using 3.25mm needles, cast on 57 (57, 79, 101,
112) sts and commencing with row 1 work 3
repeats of lace pattern (54 rows in total). Work 0 (0,
0, 8, 8) more rows in lace pattern.

All sizes
Shape Sleeve Head
Maintaining pattern, cast off 3 (3, 3, 5, 6) sts at beg of next 2 (2, 4, 4, 4) rows, 51 (51, 67, 81, 88) sts. Dec 1 st at each end of 4 (2, 16, 24, 25) foll alt rows, then on 8 (10, 4, 1, 2) foll 4th rows, 27 (27, 27, 31, 34) sts rem. Cast off rem sts.

MAKING UP
Block work to specified dimensions. Join shoulder seams.

NECK BAND
With RS facing, using 3.25mm circular needle and commencing at back neck, K across 35 (35, 43, 45, 47) sts on holder, pick up and K 24 (24, 24, 26, 26) sts down left side neck, K across 13 (13, 15, 17, 19) sts from front neck, and pick up and K 24 (24, 24, 26, 26) sts up right side neck, 96 (96, 106, 114, 118) sts.

Round 1: K.
Round 2: P.
Round 3: As round 1.
Round 4: As round 2.
Cast off knitwise loosely.

Sew up side and sleeve seams. Insert sleeves and sew into place, taking care to match centre of sleeve head with shoulder seam and matching side seams, easing in remaining fabric. Darn in all ends.

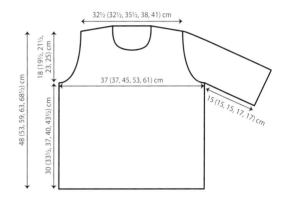

On a trip to Australia in the early 1950s, Elizabeth wore what is considered by many to be the most glamorous outfit she ever wore. A 'wiggle' dress in white lace designed by Hardy Amies, it was perfect for Australia's heat and looked young, fresh and a little sexy!

I was inspired to create a knitted 'homage' to this amazing dress. I designed a short-sleeved top in white lambswool, using a simple repeating lace pattern, with negative ease to create a similar fit to Elizabeth's wiggle dress. I found the lace design being used on a design in a 1950s Woman's Weekly which seemed very appropriate. The lambswool is very lightweight and the lace airy giving a look not dissimilar to her dress. It seemed only fitting to name it after the great British designer, Hardy Amies himself.

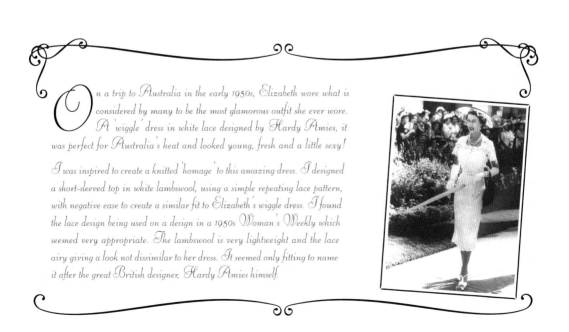

I've been to London to visit the Queen

MATERIALS

Cygnet Truly Wool Rich 4 ply, 75% pure new superwash wool, 25% polyamide (205m per 50g)
7 (8, 8, 9, 10, 11, 11) balls, shade 2151 (Raspberry) – used double throughout
4 button moulds
Approx 1m (1yd) length of contrast fabric
Sewing needle and thread

TENSION

24 sts & 28 rows = 10cm (4in) using 3.75mm needles over twisted stitch pattern

ABBREVIATIONS

See page 95

SIZING

To fit Chest	cm	53	55	58½	60	63½	65	67
	(in)	(20¾)	(21¾)	(23)	(23½)	(25)	(25½)	(26½)
To fit Age		2	3	4	5	6	7	8
Actual Chest Size	cm	56	57½	59	62½	66	67½	69
	(in)	(22)	(22¾)	(23¼)	(24½)	(26)	(26½)	(27¼)
Length to Underarm	cm	33	34½	35½	36½	38	41½	43
	(in)	(13)	(13½)	(14)	(14¼)	(15)	(16¼)	(17)
Armhole Depth	cm	10½	11½	12	12	12½	13	14
	(in)	(4¼)	(4½)	(4¾)	(4¾)	(5)	(5)	(5½)
Finished Length	cm	43½	46	47½	48½	50½	54½	57
	(in)	(17¼)	(18)	(18¾)	(19)	(20)	(21½)	(22½)
Sleeve Length	cm	21½	24	26½	27½	29	30	31½
	(in)	(8½)	(9½)	(10½)	(10¾)	(11½)	(11¾)	(12½)
Shoulder to Shoulder	cm	24½	24½	25½	25½	26½	26½	27
	(in)	(9¾)	(9¾)	(10)	(10)	(10¼)	(10¼)	(10¾)

Sample size shown to fit age 2 (53cm chest, 92cm height)

PATTERN NOTES

Yarn is used doubled throughout

BACK

Using 3.75mm needles and yarn doubled, cast on 99 (101, 103, 107, 111, 113, 115) sts and commence working as folls:

Foundation row (WS): K.

Row 1 (RS): K0 (1, 2, 0, 2, 3, 0), [T2, K2] 12 (12, 12, 13, 13, 13, 14) times, P3, [T2, K2] 12 (12, 12, 13, 13, 13, 14) times, K0 (1, 2, 0, 2, 3, 0).

Row 2: P48 (49, 50, 52, 54, 55, 56), K3, P48 (49, 50, 52, 54, 55, 56).

Row 3: K0 (1, 2, 0, 2, 3, 0), [K2, T2] 12 (12, 12, 13, 13, 13, 14) times, P3, [K2, T2] 12 (12, 12, 13, 13, 13, 14) times, K0 (1, 2, 0, 2, 3, 0).

Row 4: As row 2.

These 4 rows form pattern. Rep patt a further 3 times (16 rows worked in total).

SHAPE SKIRT

Dec row: K2tog, patt 44 (45, 46, 48, 50, 51, 52) sts, K2tog, P3, K2tog, patt 44 (45, 46, 48, 50, 51, 52) sts, K2tog, 95 (97, 99, 103, 107, 109, 111) sts. Continue in pattern, keeping centre 3 sts in reverse stocking stitch, dec 4 sts as set on 7 foll 8th rows, 67 (69, 71, 75, 79, 81, 83) sts. Continue in pattern without further shaping until work measures 33 (34½, 35½, 36½, 38, 41½, 43) cm (13, 13½, 14, 14¼, 15, 16¼, 17 in) ending with a WS row.

Shape Armholes

Maintaining pattern, cast off 3 sts at beg of next 2 (2, 2, 4, 4, 4, 4) rows, 61 (63, 65, 63, 67, 69, 71) sts. Dec 1 st at each end of 1 (2, 2, 1, 2, 3, 3) foll rows, 59 (59, 61, 61, 63, 63, 65) sts. Work without further shaping until armhole measures 10½ (11½, 12, 12, 12½, 13, 14) cm (4¼, 4½, 4¾, 4¾, 5, 5, 5½ in) ending with a WS row.

Shape Shoulders

Maintaining pattern, cast off 10 (10, 10, 10, 11, 11, 11) sts at beg of next 4 rows, 19 (19, 21, 21, 19, 19, 21) sts. Leave rem sts on holder.

RIGHT FRONT

Using 3.75mm needles and yarn doubled, cast on 64 (65, 66, 68, 70, 71, 72) sts and commence working as folls:

Foundation row (WS): K.

Row 1 (RS): K1, [T2, K2] 6 times, P3, [T2, K2] 9 (9, 9, 10, 10, 10, 11) times, K0 (1, 2, 0, 2, 3, 0).

Row 2: P36 (37, 38, 40, 42, 43, 44), K3, P25.

Row 3: K1, [K2, T2] 6 times, P3, [K2, T2] 9 (9, 9, 10, 10, 10, 11) times, K0 (1, 2, 0, 2, 3, 0).

Row 4: As row 2.

These 4 rows form pattern. Rep patt a further 3 times (16 rows worked in total).

Shape Skirt

Dec row (RS): Patt 23, K2tog, P3, K2tog, patt 32 (33, 34, 36, 38, 39, 40), K2tog, 61 (62, 63, 65, 67, 68, 69) sts.

Continue in pattern, keeping 3 sts in reverse stocking stitch, dec 3 sts as set on 7 foll 8th rows, 40 (41, 42, 44, 46, 47, 48) sts, and AT THE SAME TIME when 60 (60, 64, 66, 66, 72, 72) rows have been worked from cast on edge work buttonhole as folls:

Buttonhole row (RS): Patt 2, cast off 3, patt to end.
Next row: Patt to cast off sts, cast on 3, patt 2.
Continue in pattern, completing side shaping if necessary, and work a further buttonhole on the foll 15th & 16th (17th & 18th, 17th & 18th, 17th & 18th, 19th & 20th, 21st & 22nd, 23rd & 24th) rows. Work straight until piece measures same as Back to armhole shaping, ending with a RS row.

Shape Armhole

Maintaining pattern, cast off 3 sts at beg of next and 0 (0, 0, 1, 1, 1, 1) foll alt row, 37 (38, 39, 38, 40, 41, 42) sts. Work buttonhole as above on next two rows, and AT THE SAME TIME dec 1 st at beg of 1 (2, 2, 1, 2, 3, 3) foll rows, 36 (36, 37, 37, 38, 38, 39) sts. Work without further shaping until armhole measures 15 (15, 15, 15, 17, 17, 17) rows less than back to commencement of shoulder shaping, ending with a WS row.

Row 1 (RS): Patt 17 sts, purl to end.
Row 2 (WS): K19 (19, 20, 20, 21, 21, 22) sts, patt to end.
Row 3: As row 1.
Row 4: P.
Row 5: Patt 2, cast off 3, cont in twisted st patt only to end of row.
Row 6: P to cast off sts, cast on 3, P to end.
Row 7: Twisted st patt over all sts.
Row 8: P.

Now continue in twisted st patt across all sts.

Shape Neck

Row 9 (RS): Cast off 10 (10, 11, 11, 8, 8, 9) sts, patt to end, 26 (26, 26, 26, 30, 30, 30) sts. Maintaining patt, dec 1 st at neck edge of next 6 (6, 6, 6, 8, 8, 8) rows, 20 (20, 20, 20, 22, 22, 22 sts).

Shape Shoulder

Maintaining patt, cast off 10 (10, 10, 10, 11, 11, 11) sts at beg of next and foll alt row.

LEFT FRONT

Using 3.75mm needles and yarn doubled, cast on 64 (65, 66, 68, 70, 71, 72) sts and commence working as folls:
Foundation row (WS): K.
Row 1 (RS): K0 (1, 2, 0, 2, 3, 0), [K2, T2] 9 (9, 9, 10, 10, 10, 11) times, P3, [K2, T2] 6 times, K1.

Row 2: P25, K3, P36 (37, 38, 40, 42, 43, 44).
Row 3: K0 (1, 2, 0, 2, 3, 0), [T2, K2] 9 (9, 9, 10, 10, 10, 11) times, P3, [T2, K2] 6 times, K1.
Row 4: As row 2.
These 4 rows form pattern. Rep patt a further 3 times (16 rows worked in total).

Shape Skirt

Dec row (RS): K2tog, patt 32 (33, 34, 36, 38, 39, 40), K2tog, P3, K2tog, patt 23, 61 (62, 63, 65, 67, 68, 69) sts.

Continue in pattern, keeping 3 sts in reverse stocking stitch, dec 3 sts as set on 7 foll 8th rows, 40 (41, 42, 44, 46, 47, 48) sts. Continue in pattern until piece measures same as Back to armhole shaping, ending with a WS row.

Shape Armhole

Maintaining pattern, cast off 3 sts at beg of next and 0 (0, 0, 1, 1, 1, 1) foll alt row, 37 (38, 39, 38, 40, 41, 42) sts. Work 1 row straight. Dec 1 st at beg of 1 (2, 2, 1, 2, 3, 3) foll rows, 36 (36, 37, 37, 38, 38, 39 sts). Work without further shaping until armhole measures 14 (14, 14, 14, 16, 16, 16) rows less than back to commencement of shoulder shaping, ending with a WS row.

Row 1 (RS): P19 (19, 20, 20, 21, 21, 22), patt to end.
Row 2 (WS): P17, K to end.
Row 3: P19 (19, 20, 20, 21, 21, 22), patt to end.
Row 4: P.
Row 5: Work in twisted st patt across all sts.
Row 6: P.
Row 7: Work in twisted st patt across all sts.

Now continue in twisted st patt across all sts.

Shape Neck

Row 8 (WS): Cast off 10 (10, 11, 11, 8, 8, 9) sts, patt to end, 26 (26, 26, 26, 30, 30, 30) sts. Maintaining patt, dec 1 st at neck edge of next 6 (6, 6, 6, 8, 8, 8) rows, 20 (20, 20, 20, 22, 22, 22 sts).

Shape Shoulder

Maintaining patt, cast off 10 (10, 10, 10, 11, 11, 11) sts at beg of next and foll alt row.

SLEEVES

Using 3.75mm needles and yarn doubled, cast on 40 (42, 44, 46, 48, 50, 52) sts and commence working as folls:

Foundation row (WS): K.

Row 1 (RS): [K2, T2] 10 (10, 11, 11, 12, 12, 13) times, K0 (2, 0, 2, 0, 2, 0).

Row 2 (WS): P.

Row 3: [T2, K2] 10 (10, 11, 11, 12, 12, 13) times, [T2] 0 (1, 0, 1, 0, 1, 0) time.

Row 4: As row 2.

These 4 rows set twisted stitch pattern. Work another 10 rows in pattern as set, then taking inc sts into pattern, inc 1 st at each end of next and 6 foll 6th (8th, 8th, 8th, 8th, 10th, 10th) rows, 54 (56, 58, 60, 62, 64, 66) sts.

Work without further shaping until sleeve measures 21½ (24, 26½, 27½, 29, 30, 31½) cm (8½, 9½, 10½, 10¾, 11½, 11¾, 12½ in) ending with a WS row.

Shape Sleeve Head

Maintaining pattern cast off 3 sts at beg of next 2 (2, 2, 4, 4, 4, 4) rows, 48 (50, 52, 48, 50, 52, 54) sts. Dec 1 st at each end of next and 3 (4, 5, 5, 6, 5, 8) foll alt rows, 42 (42, 42, 38, 38, 42, 38) sts. Dec 1 st at each end of every row until 14 sts rem. Cast off rem sts.

MAKING UP

Press all pieces on WS of work.

COLLAR

Using a single strand of yarn, join shoulder seams then with WS of work facing, pick up and K 23 (23, 23, 23, 22, 22, 23) sts across right front neck, commencing approx 1½cm (½in) from front edge, K across 9 (9, 10, 10, 9, 9, 10) sts at back neck, Kfb, K across rem 9 (9, 10, 10, 9, 9, 10) sts at back neck, then pick up and K 23 (23, 23, 23, 22, 22, 23) sts across left front neck, ending approx 1½cm (½in) from front edge, 66 (66, 68, 68, 64, 64, 68) sts.

5th and 6th sizes only

Next row: K10, (Kfb) twice, K40, (Kfb) twice, K10, (68 sts).

Next row: P.

All sizes

Commencing with a K row, work in stocking stitch for 16 (16, 16, 16, 16, 16, 18) rows (reverse stocking stitch is the RS of the collar).

Cast off loosely.

Using a single strand of yarn, join side and sleeve seams. Insert sleeves into armholes taking care to match centre of sleeve head with shoulder seam. Darn in all ends.

Cut four small squares from contrast fabric large enough to cover button moulds. Work running stitch around the edges and draw up around the button mould. Fasten off securely and then clip on back of button mould.

Place collar onto contrast fabric and draw carefully round outer edge. Allow a small seam allowance all round and then cut out fabric. With RS together pin fabric to collar around outer edge and then backstitch firmly around this edge. Turn fabric over so that it is now on the underside of the collar with WS together. Press on underside of collar, turning over lower edge of collar to WS, then pin lower edge in position to back neck and then slip stitch in place.

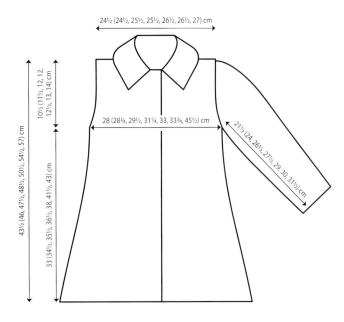

Cut two strips of fabric the same length as coat centre fronts and approx 7½cm (3in) wide. Pin strips to centre front edges of jacket with RS together. Backstitch firmly, close to edges. Turn fabric over so that it is now on the underside of the front edges of the jacket. Press edging on underside, turning over unfinished edges of fabric strip to WS at same time. Pin remaining edges in position and then slip stitch in place.

Tack around each buttonhole through both knitted and woven fabric, holding the fabric strip in position, then using a seam ripper if possible, or fine sharp needlework scissors cut open the woven fabric through the buttonhole. Neaten hole and then work buttonhole stitch through both layers of fabric from the RS of the work. Sew buttons in place. Press again on RS of work through a damp cloth.

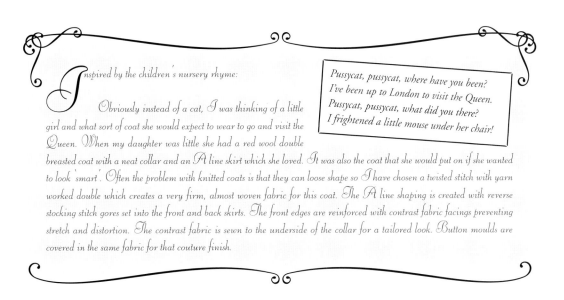

Inspired by the children's nursery rhyme:

Obviously instead of a cat, I was thinking of a little girl and what sort of coat she would expect to wear to go and visit the Queen. When my daughter was little she had a red wool double breasted coat with a neat collar and an A line skirt which she loved. It was also the coat that she would put on if she wanted to look 'smart'. Often the problem with knitted coats is that they can loose shape so I have chosen a twisted stitch with yarn worked double which creates a very firm, almost woven fabric for this coat. The A line shaping is created with reverse stocking stitch gores set into the front and back skirts. The front edges are reinforced with contrast fabric facings preventing stretch and distortion. The contrast fabric is sewn to the underside of the collar for a tailored look. Button moulds are covered in the same fabric for that couture finish.

Pussycat, pussycat, where have you been?
I've been up to London to visit the Queen.
Pussycat, pussycat, what did you there?
I frightened a little mouse under her chair!

Coronation Sleeveless Pullover

MATERIALS

Jamieson & Smith 2 Ply Jumper Weight 100% Shetland wool
(115m / 125yds per 25g ball)

7 (8, 10, 12, 14, 16) balls shade FC47 – MC

4 (5, 6, 7, 8, 10) balls shade 01A – CC

– or –

Excelana Luxury 4 Ply Wool 100% pure new British wool
(159m / 174yds per 50g ball)

6 (7, 8, 9, 11, 12) balls shade Cornflower Blue – MC

3 (4, 5, 6, 7, 8) ball shade Alabaster – CC

1 pair 2.75mm (US #2) needles
1 pair 3.25mm (US #3) needles

– or –

1 2.75mm (US #2) circular needle (60cm)
1 3.25mm (US #3) circular needle (60cm)

A set of 2.75mm (US #2) double pointed needles
or 2.75mm (US #2) circular needle (40cm long)

Waste yarn
Stitch markers
Spare needles

TENSION

29 sts & 30 rows = 10cm (4in) using 3.25mm needles
measured over Fair Isle pattern after blocking

1 patt rep (36 sts and 32 rows) measures 12 × 10½ cm
(4¾ × 4 in) after blocking

ABBREVIATIONS

See page 95

SIZING

To Fit	cm	81	97	107	117	132	142
	(in)	(32)	(38)	(42)	(46)	(52)	(56)
Actual Chest Size	cm	87	99½	111½	124	136½	149
	(in)	(34¼)	(39)	(44)	(48¾)	(53¾)	(58¾)
Length to Underarm	cm	35½	39½	43	47	51	55
	(in)	(14)	(15½)	(16¾)	(18½)	(20)	(21½)
Armhole Depth	cm	20	21½	23½	24½	26	27½
	(in)	(7¾)	(8½)	(9¼)	(9¾)	(10¼)	(10¾)
Finished Length	cm	55½	61	66	71½	77	82
	(in)	(21¾)	(24)	(26)	(28¼)	(30¼)	(32¼)
Shoulder to Shoulder	cm	32½	35	40	45	49	51½
	(in)	(12¾)	(13¾)	(15¾)	(17¾)	(19¼)	(20¼)
Back Neck Width	cm	14½	16½	17	20	22	23
	(in)	(5¾)	(6½)	(6¾)	(7¾)	(8¾)	(9)

Model is shown wearing size to fit chest 97cm (38in)

PATTERN NOTES

Pattern instructions are included to either knit this
garment in the round or to knit the front and back
as separate pieces and then sew together.

Worked in the Round

BODY

Cast on 252 (288, 324, 360, 396, 432) sts using 2.75mm circular needle and MC. Join into a round, taking care not to twist sts. Place marker at join (this marker denotes right seam position).

Round 1: * K1, P1, rep from * to end of round, placing marker after 126 (144, 162, 180, 198, 216) sts have been worked (this marker denotes left seam position).
Continue in rib as set until work measures 7½cm (3in).
Change to 3.25mm circular needle.

Round 1: Reading from right to left on row 1 of chart A (B, A, B, A, B), repeat 36-stitch motif 7 (8, 9, 10, 11, 12) times to end of round.
Cont to work from chart A (B, A, B, A, B) as set until 85 (97, 107, 119, 131, 143) rounds of colourwork have been completed. 2 (3, 3, 3, 4, 4) whole repeats and 21 (1, 11, 23, 3, 15) rows of the charted pattern, and if row tension is correct, garment should measure 35½ (39½, 43, 47, 51, 55) cm (14, 15½, 16¾, 18½, 20, 21½ in).

Shape Armholes

Next round: Keeping chart pattern correct, patt 119 (135, 153, 174, 191, 208) sts, cast off next 14 (18, 18, 12, 14, 16) sts, patt until you have 112 (126, 144, 168, 184, 200) sts on right needle after cast off sts, then cast off following 14 (18, 18, 12, 14, 16) sts (this will be 7 (9, 9, 6, 7, 8) sts from each side of the start of round marker).
You will now have two sets of 112 (126, 144, 168, 184, 200) sts. The first set are back sts, and the second set are front sts.

Work back and forth on back sts only (WS rows will be purled and read from left to right on the chart):

4th, 5th and 6th sizes only

Keeping chart pattern correct, cast off (6, 7, 8) sts at beg of next 2 rows (156, 170, 184) sts.

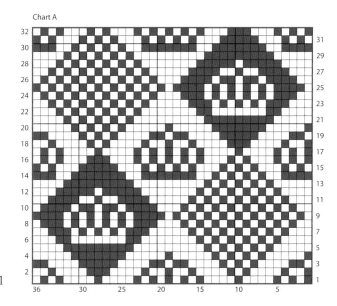

Chart A

Chart B

Key

- ■ MC (FC47); Knit on RS, Purl on WS
- □ CC (01A); Knit on RS, Purl on WS
- ☐ Pattern repeat

All sizes

Working in chart pattern as set throughout, dec 1 st at each end of 5 (7, 7, 7, 9, 11) following rows, 102 (112, 130, 142, 152, 162) sts, then dec 1 st at each end of 3 (4, 6, 5, 4, 5) foll alt rows, 96 (104, 118, 132, 144, 152) sts and then dec 1 st at each end of foll 4th row, 94 (102, 116, 130, 142, 150) sts.

Now work straight in colourwork pattern, until in total, 144 (160, 176, 192, 208, 224) rows have been worked in charted pattern. 4 (5, 5, 6, 6, 7) whole repeats and 16 (0, 16, 0, 16, 0) rows of the charted pattern, and if row tension is correct, garment should measure 55½ (61, 66, 71½, 77, 82) cm (21¾, 24, 26, 28¼, 30¼, 32¼ in).

Place 26 (27, 33, 36, 39, 42) sts onto a spare needle for right shoulder, then place centre 42 (48, 50, 58, 64, 66) sts on a holder for back neck, and place rem 26 (27, 33, 36, 39, 42) sts onto a second spare needle for left shoulder.

FRONT

With RS facing, rejoin yarn to 112 (126, 144, 168, 184, 200) sts for front. Starting on chart row 23 (3, 13, 25, 5, 17), continue as folls:

4th, 5th and 6th sizes only

Keeping chart pattern correct, cast off (6, 7, 8) sts at beg of next 2 rows (156, 170, 184) sts.

***Working in chart pattern as set throughout, dec 1 st at each end of 5 (6, 6, 4, 4, 4) following rows, 102 (114, 132, 148, 162, 176) sts. Work 1 (0, 0, 0, 0, 0) row without shaping, thus ending with RS facing for next row.

Next row (RS): Patt2tog, patt 47 (53, 62, 70, 77, 84) sts, K2tog, turn, leaving rem 51 (57, 66, 74, 81, 88) sts on a stitch holder for right neck.

Next row: Pattern to last 0 (0, 0, 2, 2, 2) sts, Patt2tog, 0 (0, 0, 1, 1, 1) time, 49 (55, 64, 71, 78, 85) sts.

Dec 1 st at neck edge of next and 19 (22, 23, 27, 30, 31) foll alt rows AND AT THE SAME TIME, dec 1 st at armhole edge of foll 1 (1, 1, 1, 3, 5) rows, then dec 1 st at armhole edge of foll 1 (3, 5, 5, 4, 5) alt rows, and then dec 1 st at armhole edge of foll 4th row, 26 (27, 33, 36, 39, 42) sts. Work straight until front matches back to shoulder.***

With RS facing, rejoin yarn to 51 (57, 66, 74, 81, 88) sts on holder for right neck and work as folls, commencing at chart row 29 (9, 19, 29, 11, 23):
Next row (RS): Patt2tog, patt 47 (53, 62, 70, 77, 84) sts, K2tog.

Next row (WS): Patt2tog, 0 (0, 0, 1, 1, 1) time, patt to end, 49 (55, 64, 71, 78, 85) sts.
Complete to match first side and join front and back shoulders using a three needle cast off.

MAKING UP

ARM BANDS

Starting at centre of underarm and with RS facing, using 2.75mm circular needle or DPNs and MC, pick up and knit 65 (71, 75, 83, 89, 95) sts to shoulder seam, then pick up and knit 65 (71, 75, 83, 89, 95) sts back round to centre underarm, 130 (142, 150, 166, 178, 190) sts. Join into a round and place marker for start of round.

Next round: * K1, P1, rep from * to end of round.
Last round sets rib. Continue to work in rib until armband measures 2½cm (1in). Cast off all sts in rib. Repeat for other side.

NECK BAND

Commencing at left shoulder seam, with RS facing, using 2.75mm circular needle or DPNs and MC, pick up and knit 54 (58, 62, 68, 74, 78) sts to centre of V-neck, pick up and knit 1 st at centre, pick up and knit 55 (59, 63, 69, 75, 79) sts to right shoulder seam, then pick up and knit 42 (48, 50, 58, 64, 66) sts across back neck, 152 (166, 176, 196, 214, 224) sts.

Round 1: * K1, P1, rep from * 26 (28, 30, 33, 36, 38) more times, PM, K1, PM, * P1, K1, rep from * to last st, P1.

Round 2: Work in rib as set to 2 sts before marker, Sl1, K1, psso, SM, K1, SM, K2tog, work in rib as set to end of round.

Round 3: Work in rib as set to marker, SM, K1, SM, work in rib as set to end of round.
Repeat last 2 rounds until neckband measures 3cm (1¼in).
Cast off all sts in rib.

Spray garment with cold water and press to required measurements.
Darn in all ends.

Worked Flat

BACK

Cast on 126 (144, 162, 180, 198, 216) sts using 2.75mm needles and MC.
Row 1 (RS): * K1, P1, rep from * to end.
Row 2 (WS): As row 1.
These 2 rows set rib. Cont to work in rib until piece measures 7½cm (3in) ending with a WS row.

Change to 3.25mm needles.
Row 1 (RS): Reading from right to left on row 1 of chart A (B, A, B, A, B), start at stitch 19 (1, 19, 1, 19, 1) and work to st 36 once, then repeat the marked 36-stitch motif 3 (3, 4, 4, 5, 5) times, thus ending at stitch 36.

Row 2 (WS): Reading from left to right on row 2 of chart A (B, A, B, A, B), start at stitch 36 and work the marked repeat 3 (3, 4, 4, 5, 5) times, then work from stitch 36 to stitch 9 (1, 19, 1, 19, 1) once.
Cont to work from chart A (B, A, B, A, B) as set until 84 (96, 106, 118, 130, 142) rows of colourwork have been completed. 2 (3, 3, 3, 4, 4) whole repeats and 20 (0, 10, 22, 2, 14) rows of the charted pattern, and if row tension is correct, garment should measure 35½ (39½, 43, 47, 51, 55) cm (14, 15½, 16¾, 18½, 20, 21½ in).

Shape Armhole

Keeping colourwork pattern correct throughout, cast off 7 (9, 9, 6, 7, 8) sts at beg of next 2 (2, 2, 4, 4, 4) rows, 112 (126, 144, 156, 170, 184) sts.**
Dec 1 st at each end of 5 (7, 7, 7, 9, 11) rows, 102 (112, 130, 142, 152, 162) sts.
Dec 1 st at each end of 3 (4, 6, 5, 4, 5) foll alt rows, 96 (104, 118, 132, 144, 152) sts.
Dec 1 st at each end of foll 4th row, 94 (102, 116, 130, 142, 150) sts.

Chart A

Chart B

Key
- ■ MC (FC47); Knit on RS, Purl on WS
- □ CC (01A); Knit on RS, Purl on WS
- □ Pattern repeat

Now work straight in colourwork pattern, until in total, 144 (160, 176, 192, 208, 224) rows have been worked in charted pattern. 4 (5, 5, 6, 6, 7) whole repeats and 16 (0, 16, 0, 16, 0) rows of the charted pattern, and if row tension is correct, garment should measure 55½ (61, 66, 71½, 77, 82) cm (21¾, 24, 26, 28¼, 30¼, 32¼ in).
Cast off all stitches.

FRONT

Work as for back to **.

Work as for front, in the round instructions from *** to ***, 26 (27, 33, 36, 39, 42) sts.

Cast off rem sts.

Complete second side of front neck to match first, as per in the round instructions, casting off all stitches when complete.

MAKING UP

Join right shoulder seam.

NECK BAND

Commencing at left shoulder, with RS facing, using 2.75mm needles and MC, pick up and knit 54 (58, 62, 68, 74, 78) sts to centre of V-neck, pick up and knit 1 st at centre, pick up and knit 54 (58, 62, 68, 74, 78) sts to right shoulder seam, then pick up and knit 42 (48, 50, 58, 64, 66) sts across back neck, 151 (165, 175, 195, 213, 223) sts.

Row 1 (WS): * P1, K1, rep from * 47 (52, 55, 62, 68, 71) more times, PM, P1, PM, * K1, P1, rep from * to end.

Row 2 (RS): Work in rib as set to 2 sts before marker, Sl1, K1, psso, SM, K1, SM, K2tog, work in rib as set to end of row.

Row 3: Work in rib as set to marker, SM, P1, SM, work in rib as set to end.

Repeat last 2 rows until neckband measures 3cm (1¼in).

Cast off all sts in rib.

ARM BANDS

Join left shoulder and neckband seam.

Starting at underarm and with RS facing, using 2.75mm needles and MC, pick up and knit 65 (71, 75, 83, 89, 95) sts to shoulder seam, pick up and knit 1 st in shoulder seam, then pick up and knit 65 (71, 75, 83, 89, 95) sts back down to underarm, 131 (143, 151, 167, 179, 191) sts.

Row 1 (WS): * P1, K1, rep from * to last st, P1.

Row 2 (RS): * K1, P1, rep from * to last st, K1.

Last 2 rows set rib. Continue to work in rib until armband measures 2½cm (1in). Cast off all sts in rib.

Repeat for other side.

Join side and armband seams. Spray garment with cold water and press to required measurements. Darn in all ends.

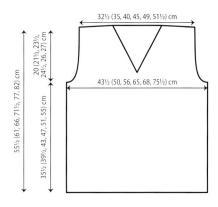

When putting together my ideas for this book I really wanted to include a man's traditional 1940s/50s sleeveless pullover but with a new motif. I drew numerous images of all manner of symbols until finally coming up with the idea of this simple crown motif. Using it throughout the garment and simply reversing the colours from cream on blue to blue on cream makes for a very enjoyable knit. Half way through the first repeat the pattern becomes automatic and the knitting very easy to read. The instructions are provided for both knitting the slipover in the round or flat in two pieces — as it would very likely have been written in the 1950s. The first size is small enough for a 32 inch chest so either a young teen or it could even be classed as unisex. I love everything about this design and in particular I love that it's the perfect garment for piloting a boat, a fast car or a plane or for smoking a pipe while building a matchstick model of a cathedral.

Silk Rose

MATERIALS

Fyberspates Scrumptious Lace, 45% Silk, 55% Merino,
(1000m / 1093yds per 100g skein)
1 skein each of:
Natural – MC
Cherry – CC1
Rose Pink – CC2
Oyster – CC3
Wine Gum – CC4
1 set 3mm (US #2–3) long double pointed needles (DPNs)

1 3mm (US #2–3) circular needle, 80cm length
Stitch markers
1 3mm crochet hook
A small quantity of 4ply waste yarn

TENSION
30 sts & 37 rows using 3mm needles over stocking stitch

ABBREVIATIONS
See page 95

SIZING
Finished size (after blocking) 53½cm (21in) square

PATTERN NOTES
The floral central panel of the scarf is knitted first
using long dpns. The panel is knitted flat using
intarsia technique and is shown in its entirety on the
chart. It is advisable to prepare several small balls of
each colour before commencing knitting. Once the
central panel is completed the circular needle is used
to pick up stitches on all four sides of the panel and
then work continues in the round. The scarf is
designed to be square and this is achieved during the
blocking phase when the four 'corners' are pinned out.

CENTRE PANEL
Using waste yarn and 3mm crochet hook, cast on
81 sts onto a 3mm dpn thus creating a provisional
cast on. Place a marker at the end of this row and
break off waste yarn. Using 3mm dpns, MC and
commencing with a K row, work 2 rows in stocking
stitch. Now working in st st throughout, commence
with row 1 of chart, reading from right to left and
using separate smalls balls of yarn for each
differently coloured section.

Next row (WS): Reading from left to right work
row 2 of chart.
Continue working from chart until all 80 rows have
been completed.
Now using MC only, and commencing with a K
row, work 2 rows in stocking stitch.

Change to 3mm circular needle and CC2.
Work as folls:
With RS facing, K across 80 sts on dpn, then pick
up and K 80 sts evenly along first side of panel.
Carefully undo provisional cast on, commencing at
end with marker attached, placing the 80 live sts
from the bottom edge of the panel onto a spare dpn.
Please note there is always one less st after a
provisional cast on has been removed. K across these
80 sts then pick up and K 80 sts evenly along
second side of panel (320 sts). Place marker to
indicate end of round.
Next round: * Kfb, K to last st before marker, Kfb,
SM, rep from * to end of round (328 sts).
Next round: K.

Key

- ☐ MC (Natural); Knit on RS, Purl on WS
- ■ CC1 (Cherry); Knit on RS, Purl on WS
- ▨ CC2 (Rose Pink); Knit on RS, Purl on WS
- ☐ CC3 (Oyster); Knit on RS, Purl on WS
- ■ CC4 (Wine Gum); Knit on RS, Purl on WS

Rep these 2 rounds once more (336 sts).

Change to CC3 and rep last 2 rounds twice more (352 sts).

Change to CC4 and rep these 2 rounds twice more (368 sts).

Change to MC and repeat these 2 rounds once more (376 sts) then the first round only once more again (384 sts).

Now commence feather stitch lace edging as folls:

Round 1: * K3 [K3, YO, K1, YO, K3, K3tog] 9 times, K3, SM, rep from * to end of round.

Round 2: * Kfb, K to last st before marker, Kfb, SM, rep from * to end of round (392sts).

Round 3: * K5 [K3, YO, K1, YO, K3, K3tog] 9 times, K3, SM, rep from * to end of round.

Round 4: As round 2 (400 sts).

Round 5: * K7 [K3, YO, K1, YO, K3, K3tog] 9 times, K3, SM, rep from * to end of round.

Round 6: as round 2 (408 sts).

Change to CC1 and continue as folls:
Round 7: * K9 [K3, YO, K1, YO, K3, K3tog] 9 times, K3, SM, rep from * to end of round.
Round 8: As round 2 (416 sts).
Round 9: * K1 [K3, YO, K1, YO, K3, K3tog] 10 times, K3, SM, rep from * to end of round.
Round 10: As round 2 (424 sts).
Round 11: * K3 [K3, YO, K1, YO, K3, K3tog] 10 times, K3, SM, rep from * to end of round.
Round 12: As round 2 (432 sts).
Round 13: * K5 [K3, YO, K1, YO, K3, K3tog] 10 times, K3, SM, rep from * to end of round.
Round 14: As round 2 (440 sts).
Round 15: * K7 [K3, YO, K1, YO, K3, K3tog] 10 times, K3, SM, rep from * to end of round.
Round 16: As round 2 (448 sts).
Round 17: * K9 [K3, YO, K1, YO, K3, K3tog] 10 times, K3, SM, rep from * to end of round.
Round 18: As round 2 (456 sts).

These last 10 rounds (from rounds 9–18 inclusive) set pattern. Continue as set, inc 8 sts on every alt row and incorporating them into pattern on each round 9 until 496 sts and 28 rounds have been worked since lace edging commenced. If a larger scarf is preferred work additional patt reps ending with round 18. Cast off fairly loosely.

MAKING UP
Handwash scarf and gently squeeze dry. Pin scarf out to required measurements, commencing with the centre panel, carefully pinning out corners to create square. When outer edge reached pin out corners and then pin out feather stitch points. When scarf is dry remove pins and darn in all ends carefully.

There couldn't be a collection of designs with a connection to HRH without a headscarf. I too have a bit of a thing about head scarves and have a large collection of vintage silk scarves. With Silk Rose this is what I wanted to recreate but in knitting. I therefore chose a laceweight silk and merino yarn to produce a very light and soft fabric. Roughly square in shape, the central rose panel is knitted first using combined Fair Isle and Intarsia colourwork. Stitches are then picked up around all four sides of the panel onto a circular needle and the inner border is worked in the round. Finally a lace edging is worked right around the scarf before casting off. The lightness of the scarf also makes it perfect for wearing under a coat or jacket or over a jumper for decorative effect — or of course, for walking the corgis.

Princess Twinset Cardigan

MATERIALS

Excelana 4 Ply Luxury Wool 100% pure new British wool (159m / 174yds per 50g ball)
6 (7, 8, 8, 9, 9, 10, 11, 11, 12, 13) balls
shade Cornflower Blue or Ruby Red (as shown on page 3)
1 pair 2.75mm (US #2) needles
1 pair 3mm (US #2–3) needles
6 buttons (optional)
6 press studs
Stitch markers

TENSION

28 sts & 36 rows = 10cm (4in) using 3mm needles over stocking stitch

TWISTED STITCH TENSION

30 sts = 10cm (4in) using 3mm needles over pattern

ABBREVIATIONS

See page 95

SIZING

To Fit	cm	76	81	86	92	97	102	107	112	117	122	127
	(in)	(30)	(32)	(34)	(36)	(38)	(40)	(42)	(44)	(46)	(48)	(50)
Actual Bust	cm	85½	91½	95½	101½	107	111½	117	121½	127	131½	137
	(in)	(33¾)	(36)	(37¾)	(40)	(42¼)	(43¾)	(46)	(47¾)	(50)	(51¾)	(54)
Length to Underarm	cm	33	34	35	36½	38	39	40	41½	43	44	45
	(in)	(13)	(13½)	(13¾)	(14¼)	(15)	(15¼)	(15¾)	(16¼)	(17)	(17¼)	(17¾)
Armhole Depth	cm	14	15	17	17	18	18	19	19	20	20	21½
	(in)	(5½)	(6)	(6¾)	(6¾)	(7)	(7)	(7½)	(7½)	(7¾)	(7¾)	(8½)
Finished Length *Includes half saddle strip width*	cm	51	53	56	57½	60	61	63	64½	67	68	70½
	(in)	(20)	(20¾)	(22)	(22¾)	(23½)	(24)	(24¾)	(25½)	(26½)	(26¾)	(27¾)
Sleeve Length *not including reversed cuff*	cm	43½	46	47	47½	47½	48½	48½	48½	49½	50	50½
	(in)	(17)	(18¼)	(18½)	(18¾)	(18¾)	(19)	(19)	(19)	(19½)	(19¾)	(20)
Shoulder to Shoulder	cm	30½	32	34½	35	35	36½	38	38	40	40	41½
	(in)	(12)	(12¾)	(13½)	(13¾)	(13¾)	(14¼)	(15)	(15)	(15¾)	(15¾)	(16¼)
Back Neck Width	cm	15	15	17	18	18	18	19½	19½	20	20	20
	(in)	(6)	(6)	(6¾)	(7)	(7)	(7)	(7½)	(7½)	(7¾)	(7¾)	(7¾)

Model is shown wearing cardigan to fit chest size 92cm (36in)

BACK

Using 2.75mm needles, cast on 86 (92, 100, 108, 114, 122, 128, 136, 142, 150, 156) sts and work in rib as folls:

Row 1 (RS): * K1, P1, rep from * to end.

Rep this row until work measures 5 (5, 7½, 7½, 7½, 7½, 7½, 10, 10, 10, 10) cm (2, 2, 3, 3, 3, 3, 3, 4, 4, 4, 4 in) ending with a WS row.

Change to 3mm needles and work in pattern as folls:

Row 1: (RS): K15 (18, 22, 26, 29, 33, 36, 40, 43, 47, 50), PM, [P2, K4] 9 times, P2, PM, K15 (18, 22, 26, 29, 33, 36, 40, 43, 47, 50).

Row 2: P15 (18, 22, 26, 29, 33, 36, 40, 43, 47, 50), K2, [P4, K2] 9 times, P15 (18, 22, 26, 29, 33, 36, 40, 43, 47, 50).

Row 3: As row 1.

Row 4: As row 2.

Row 5: K15 (18, 22, 26, 29, 33, 36, 40, 43, 47, 50), [P2, TW4] 9 times, P2, K15 (18, 22, 26, 29, 33, 36, 40, 43, 47, 50).

Row 6: As row 2.

Rep these 6 rows twice more and AT THE SAME TIME commence shaping by inc 1 st at each end of next and 16 (17, 16, 16, 17, 16, 17, 16, 17, 16, 17) foll 4th (4th, 4th, 4th, 4th, 5th, 5th, 5th, 5th, 5th, 5th) rows, 120 (128, 134, 142, 150, 156, 164, 170, 178, 184, 192) sts.

Whilst continuing to work increases as set above, work in patt as folls:

*** Row 19**: Knit to marker (working an inc if required), remove marker, K6, place new marker, patt to 6 sts before marker, place new marker, K6, remove marker, knit to end (working an increase if required).

Row 20: Purl to marker (work inc if required), SM, patt to marker, SM, purl to end (working inc if required).

Row 21: Knit to marker (work inc if required), SM, patt to marker, SM, knit to end (working inc if required).

Work a further 15 rows in pattern as set. Repeat from * 3 more times. A total of 90 pattern rows have been worked since rib.

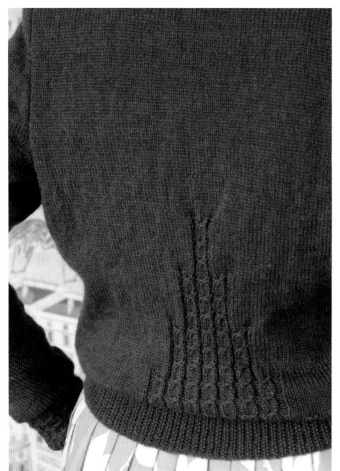

Completing increases if needed, now work in stocking stitch until piece measures 33 (34, 35, 36½, 38, 39, 40, 41½, 43, 44, 45) cm (13, 13½, 13¾, 14½, 15, 15½, 15¾, 16½, 17, 17¼, 17¾ in) ending with a WS row.

Shape Armhole
Commencing with a RS row, cast off 3 (3, 3, 4, 4, 4, 5, 5, 5, 6, 6) sts at beg of next 6 (6, 6, 6, 8, 8, 8, 8, 8, 8, 8) rows, 102 (110, 116, 118, 118, 124, 124, 130, 138, 136, 144) sts. Dec 1 st at each end of foll 8 (10, 10, 10, 10, 11, 9, 12, 13, 12, 14) rows, 86 (90, 96, 98, 98, 102, 106, 106, 112, 112, 116) sts.

Work without further shaping until armhole measures 14 (15, 17, 17, 18, 18, 19, 19, 20, 20, 21½) cm (5½, 6, 6¾, 6¾, 7, 7, 7½, 7½, 7¾, 7¾, 8½ in) ending with a WS row.
Cast off 22 (24, 24, 24, 24, 26, 26, 26, 28, 28, 30) sts at the beg of the next 2 rows.

Cast off rem 42 (42, 48, 50, 50, 50, 54, 54, 56, 56, 56) sts.

LEFT FRONT

Using 2.75mm needles, cast on 49 (51, 55, 59, 63, 67, 69, 73, 77, 81, 83) sts, and commence work as folls:

Row 1 (RS): * K1, P1, rep from * to last 9 sts, K1, P1, K4, P2, Sl1.

Row 2: P1, K2, P4, K1, P1, * K1, P1, rep from * to end.

Rep these 2 rows until work measures 5 (5, 7½, 7½, 7½, 7½, 7½, 10, 10, 10, 10) cm (2, 2, 3, 3, 3, 3, 3, 4, 4, 4, 4 in) ending with a WS row.

Change to 3mm needles and work in pattern as folls:

Row 1 (RS): K41 (43, 47, 51, 55, 59, 61, 65, 69, 73, 75), P1, K4, P2, Sl1.

Row 2: P1, K2, P4, K1, P41 (43, 47, 51, 55, 59, 61, 65, 69, 73, 75).

Row 3: As row 1.

Row 4: As row 2.

Row 5: K41 (43, 47, 51, 55, 59, 61, 65, 69, 73, 75), P1, TW4, P2, Sl1.

Row 6: As row 2.

Continue as set working twist stitch pattern at centre edge at all times, and AT SAME TIME, commence shaping by inc 1 st at beg of next and at same edge of 16 (17, 16, 16, 17, 16, 17, 16, 17, 16, 17) foll 4th (4th, 4th, 4th, 4th, 5th, 5th, 5th, 5th, 5th, 5th) rows, 66 (69, 72, 76, 81, 84, 87, 90, 95, 98, 101) sts.

Work straight until 14 rows less have been worked on front than back to start of armhole, ending with a WS row. Commence V-neck shaping as folls:

Next row (RS): K to last 10 sts, K2tog, PM, patt 8. Dec 1 st on every RS row in this manner 6 times more, 59 (62, 65, 69, 74, 77, 80, 83, 88, 91, 94) sts. P 1 row.

Before continuing to knit please read through this next section in its entirety as several actions need to be carried out at the same time.

Shape Armhole

Cast off 3 (3, 3, 4, 4, 4, 5, 5, 5, 6, 6) sts at beg of next and 2 (2, 2, 2, 3, 3, 3, 3, 3, 3, 3) foll RS rows, then dec 1 st at armhole edge on 8 (10, 10, 10, 10, 11, 9, 12, 13, 12, 14) foll rows AND AT SAME TIME, continue to work V-neck decs as set on next and 3 (0, 1, 3, 4, 4, 4, 4, 6, 6, 2) foll alt rows (these will be RS rows), and then dec 1 st at neck edge on every foll 4th row 8 (10, 12, 11, 11, 11, 12, 12, 12, 12, 15) times.

When all armhole and V-neck decreases are completed 30 (32, 32, 32, 32, 34, 34, 34, 36, 36, 38) sts will remain. Work in patt as set until front matches back to shoulder cast off edge, ending with a WS row.

Cast off 22 (24, 24, 24, 24, 26, 26, 26, 28, 28, 30) sts at beg of next row, patt rem 8 sts then place on holder. (Make a note of last row worked on 8 st border.)

Continue as set, working twist stitch pattern at centre edge at all times, and AT SAME TIME, commence shaping by inc 1 st at end of next and at same edge of 16 (17, 16, 16, 17, 16, 17, 16, 17, 16, 17) foll 4th (4th, 4th, 4th, 4th, 5th, 5th, 5th, 5th, 5th, 5th) rows, 66 (69, 72, 76, 81, 84, 87, 90, 95, 98, 101) sts.

Work straight until 13 rows less have been worked on front than back to start of armhole shaping, ending with a WS row. Commence V-neck shaping as folls:
Next row (RS): Patt 8, PM, Sl1, K1, psso, K to end. Dec 1 st on every RS row in this manner 6 times more, 59 (62, 65, 69, 74, 77, 80, 83, 88, 91, 94) sts.

Before continuing to knit please read through this next section in its entirety as several actions need to be carried out at the same time.

Shape Armhole

Cast off 3 (3, 3, 4, 4, 4, 5, 5, 5, 6, 6) sts at beg of next and 2 (2, 2, 2, 3, 3, 3, 3, 3, 3, 3) foll WS rows, then dec 1 st at armhole edge on 8 (10, 10, 10, 10, 11, 9, 12, 13, 12, 14) foll rows AND AT SAME TIME, continue to work V-neck decs as set on 4 (1, 2, 4, 5, 5, 5, 5, 7, 7, 3) foll alt rows (these will be RS rows), and then dec 1 st at neck edge on every foll 4th row 8 (10, 12, 11, 11, 11, 12, 12, 12, 12, 15) times.

When all armhole and V-neck decreases are completed 30 (32, 32, 32, 32, 34, 34, 34, 36, 36, 38) sts will remain. Work in patt as set until front matches back to shoulder cast off row, ending with a WS row.

Next row (RS): Patt 8 sts, then cast off rem 22 (24, 24, 24, 24, 26, 26, 26, 28, 28, 30) sts. Place 8 sts on holder. (Make a note of last row worked on 8 st border.)

RIGHT FRONT

Using 2.75mm needles, cast on 49 (51, 55, 59, 63, 67, 69, 73, 77, 81, 83) sts, and commence work as folls:
Row 1 (RS): Sl1, P2, K4, P1, * K1, P1, rep from * to last st, K1.
Row 2: P1, * K1, P1, rep from * to last 8 sts, K1, P4, K2, P1.
Rep these 2 rows until work measures 5 (5, 7½, 7½, 7½, 7½, 7½, 10, 10, 10, 10) cm (2, 2, 3, 3, 3, 3, 3, 4, 4, 4, 4 in) ending with a WS row.
Change to 3mm needles and work in pattern as folls:
Row 1 (RS): Sl1, P2, K4, P1, K41 (43, 47, 51, 55, 59, 61, 65, 69, 73, 75).
Row 2: P41 (43, 47, 51, 55, 59, 61, 65, 69, 73, 75), K1, P4, K2, P1.
Row 3: As row 1.
Row 4: As row 2.
Row 5: Sl1, P2, TW4, P1, K41 (43, 47, 51, 55, 59, 61, 65, 69, 73, 75).
Row 6: As row 2.

SLEEVES

Using 3mm needles, cast on 54 (54, 54, 54, 60, 60, 60, 60, 66, 66, 72) sts and work in twist stitch pattern as folls:

Row 1 (WS – cuff is turned up): [P2, K4] 9 (9, 9, 9, 10, 10, 10, 10, 11, 11, 12) times.

Row 2: [P4, K2] 9 (9, 9, 9, 10, 10, 10, 10, 11, 11, 12) times.

Row 3: As row 1.

Row 4: As row 2.

Row 5: [P2, TW4] 9 (9, 9, 9, 10, 10, 10, 10, 11, 11, 12) times.

Row 6: As row 2.

Rep these 6 rows until work measures 6½cm (2½in), ending with an even numbered row.

Change to 2.75mm needles, and work in rib as folls:

Next row: * K1, P1, rep from * to end.

Rep this row until ribbing measures 6½cm (2½in), ending with a WS row (Front of twisted stitch pattern should be facing WS).

Change to 3mm needles and commencing with a K row work in stocking stitch and AT SAME TIME, inc 1 st at each end of 5th and 1 (6, 1, 10, 14, 2, 14, 23, 24, 32, 2) foll 12th (10th, 10th, 6th, 6th, 4th, 4th, 4th, 4th, 4th, 2nd) rows, 58 (68, 58, 76, 90, 66, 90, 108, 116, 132, 78) sts. Inc 1 st at each end of 7 (5, 14, 8, 5, 20, 12, 6, 6, 1, 33) foll 14th (12th, 8th, 8th, 8th, 6th, 6th, 6th, 6th, 6th, 4th) rows, 72 (78, 86, 92, 100, 106, 114, 120, 128, 134, 144) sts.

Work without further shaping for 5cm (2in) ending with a WS row. If row tension is correct, sleeve will measure 43½ (46, 47, 47½, 47½, 48½, 48½, 48½, 49½, 50, 50½) cm (17, 18, 18½, 18¾, 18¾, 19, 19, 19, 19½, 19½, 20 in).

Shape Sleeve Head

Cast off 3 (3, 3, 4, 4, 4, 5, 5, 5, 6, 6) sts at beg of next 4 (4, 4, 4, 4, 8, 8, 8, 8, 8) rows, 60 (66, 74, 76, 84, 90, 74, 80, 88, 86, 96) sts rem, then dec 1 st at each end of next and 5 (10, 14, 17, 27, 28, 14, 19, 27, 18, 29) foll alt rows, 48 (44, 44, 40, 28, 32, 44, 40, 32, 48, 36) sts.

6th size only

Then dec 1 st at each end of every row 4 times, 24 sts.

All other sizes

Then dec 1 st at each end of every 3rd row 12 (10, 10, 8, 2, –, 10, 8, 4, 12, 6) times, 24 sts rem.

Saddle Shoulder

Commence working in patt as folls:

Row 1 (RS): P1, * K4, P2, rep from * to last 5 sts, K4, P1.

Row 2: K1, * P4, K2, rep from * to last 5 sts, P4, K1.

Row 3: As row 1.

Row 4: As row 2.

Row 5: P1, * TW4, P2, rep from * to last 5 sts, TW4, P1.

Row 6: As row 2.

These 6 rows form patt. Continue in patt until 26 (28, 28, 30, 30, 30, 30, 30, 32, 32, 34) saddle shoulder rows have been worked in total.
Cast off.

MAKING UP

Press work lightly on WS of work through damp cloth. Do not press ribs. Join saddle shoulders to back and front pieces.

NECK BAND

Using 3mm needles and with RS facing rejoin yarn to 8 sts on holder on right front and continue working in border pattern until reaches to centre back neck, ending with a WS row. Leave sts on spare needle. Now rejoin yarn to sts of left front border and work as for right front border. Graft or work three needle cast off to join bands together.

Slip stitch border into place across saddle shoulders and back neck. Sew in sleeve head then join sleeve seams taking care to sew up cuff turn back so that seam will not be visible when turned over. Join side seams. Darn in all ends.

Attach press studs to RS of left front band and on underside of right front band and sew a decorative button in place on RS of band over press studs if desired.

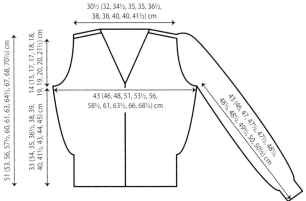

30½ (32, 34½, 35, 35, 36½, 38, 38, 40, 40, 41½) cm

43 (46, 48, 51, 53½, 56, 58½, 61, 63½, 66, 68½) cm

51 (53, 56, 57½, 60, 61, 63, 64½, 67, 68, 70½) cm

14 (15, 17, 17, 18, 18, 19, 19, 20, 20, 21½) cm

33 (34, 35, 36½, 38, 39, 40, 41½, 43, 44, 45) cm

43 (46, 47, 47½, 47½, 47½, 48½, 48½, 48½, 49½, 50, 50½) cm

Twinsets became increasingly popular through the 1940s and particularly during the 1950s, usually with a short sleeved jumper worn under a long sleeved, very slightly longer bodied cardigan. Both my grandmothers continued to wear twinsets throughout their lives and found them an irreplaceable wardrobe essential. A photograph of the princesses Elizabeth and Margaret as children show them in matching twinsets and tartan skirts very similar to those worn by my grandmothers as elderly ladies! The twisted stitch pattern on the back, front edges and saddle shoulders is echoed on the front yoke of the fitted jumper.

The shaping of the cardigan is very much a 1940s one, but if you prefer a more relaxed unfitted look you can cast on the full number of stitches needed at the bust and work straight up to the armhole shaping, remembering on the cardigan to keep your decorative twist stitch centred on the back. To ensure a perfect 1940s fit make sure that the rib band sits on your waist not the hip or the thigh by ensuring that the body length is correct for the intended wearer.

Princess Twinset Jumper

MATERIALS

Excelana 4 Ply Luxury Wool 100% pure new British wool
(159m / 174yds per 50g ball)
5 (5, 6, 6, 7, 7, 8, 8, 9, 9, 10) balls shade Alabaster
1 pair 2.75mm (US #2) needles
1 pair 3mm (US #2–3) needles
3 buttons (optional)
3 press studs
Stitch markers
Stitch holders

TENSION

28 sts & 36 rows = 10cm (4in) using 3mm needles over
stocking stitch

TWISTED STITCH TENSION

30 sts = 10cm (4in) using 3mm needles over pattern

ABBREVIATIONS

See page 95

SIZING

To Fit	cm	76	81	86	92	97	102	107	112	117	122	127
	(in)	(30)	(32)	(34)	(36)	(38)	(40)	(42)	(44)	(46)	(48)	(50)
Actual Bust Size	cm	81½	85½	91½	97	101½	107	111½	117	121½	127	131½
	(in)	(32)	(33½)	(36)	(38)	(40)	(42)	(44)	(46)	(48)	(50)	(51½)
Length to Underarm	cm	31	32	33	35	36	37	38	40	41	42	43
	(in)	(12)	(12½)	(13)	(14)	(14)	(14½)	(15)	(15½)	(16)	(16½)	(17)
Armhole Depth	cm	18½	19	21	21	22	22	23	23	24	24	25½
	(in)	(7½)	(7½)	(8½)	(8½)	(8½)	(8½)	(9)	(9)	(9½)	(9½)	(10)
Finished Length	cm	49½	51	54	56	58	59	61	63	65	66	68½
	(in)	(19½)	(20)	(21½)	(22)	(23)	(23)	(24)	(25)	(25½)	(26)	(27)
Sleeve Length	cm	15	15	15	15	15	15	15	16	16	17	18½
	(in)	(6)	(6)	(6)	(6)	(6)	(6)	(6)	(6½)	(6½)	(7)	(7)
Shoulder to Shoulder	cm	30½	32	34½	35	35	36½	38	38	40	40	41½
	(in)	(12)	(12½)	(13½)	(14)	(14)	(14½)	(15)	(15)	(15½)	(15½)	(16½)
Back Neck Width	cm	15	15	17	18	18	18	19½	19½	20	20	20
	(in)	(6)	(6)	(6½)	(7)	(7)	(7)	(7½)	(7½)	(8)	(8)	(8)

Model is shown wearing size to fit chest 76cm (30in)

BACK

Using 2.75mm needles, cast on 78 (86, 94, 102,
108, 114, 122, 130, 136, 142, 150) sts and work in
rib as folls:
Row 1 (RS): * K1, P1, rep from * to end.
Rep this row until work measures 5 (5, 5, 5, 5, 5,
7½, 7½, 7½, 7½, 7½) cm (2, 2, 2, 2, 2, 2, 3, 3, 3,
3, 3 in) ending with a WS row.
Change to 3mm needles and commencing with a K
row work in stocking stitch and AT SAME TIME,
commence shaping by inc 1 st at each end of 5th
row and then on every foll 5th (5th, 5th, 5th, 6th,
6th, 6th, 6th, 6th, 6th, 7th) row until 114 (120,
128, 136, 142, 150, 156, 164, 170, 178, 184) sts.

Continue without further shaping until work measures 31 (32, 33, 35, 36, 37, 38, 40, 41, 42, 43) cm (12, 12½, 13, 13¾, 14, 14½, 15, 15¾, 16, 16½, 17 in) ending with a WS row.

Shape Armholes

Cast off 3 (3, 3, 4, 4, 4, 5, 5, 5, 6, 6) sts at beg of next 6 (6, 6, 6, 8, 8, 8, 8, 8, 8, 8) rows 96 (102, 110, 112, 110, 118, 116, 124, 130, 130, 136) sts, then dec 1 st at each end of foll 5 (6, 7, 7, 6, 8, 5, 9, 9, 9, 10) RS rows, 86 (90, 96, 98, 98, 102, 106, 106, 112, 112, 116) sts. ***

Work without further shaping until back measures 13 (14, 16, 16, 17, 17, 18, 18, 19, 19, 20½) cm (5, 5½, 6¼, 6¼, 6¾, 6¾, 7, 7, 7½, 7½, 8in) from start of armhole shaping, ending with a WS row.

Divide for Back Neck Opening

Next row (RS): K43 (45, 48, 49, 49, 51, 53, 53, 56, 56, 58), turn, leaving rem sts on holder.

Next row (WS): Cast on 8 sts and P to end of row, 51 (53, 56, 57, 57, 59, 61, 61, 64, 64, 66) sts.

Row 1 (RS): K43 (45, 48, 49, 49, 51, 53, 53, 56, 56, 58), P1, K4, P2, Sl1.

Row 2: P1, K2, P4, K1, P43 (45, 48, 49, 49, 51, 53, 53, 56, 56, 58).

Row 3: As row 1.

Row 4: As row 2.

Row 5: K43 (45, 48, 49, 49, 51, 53, 53, 56, 56, 58), P1, TW4, P2, Sl1.

Row 6: As row 2.

These 6 rows form pattern. Continue as set until armhole measures 18½ (19, 21, 21, 22, 22, 23, 23, 24, 24, 25½) cm (7¼, 7½, 8¼, 8¼, 8½, 8½, 9, 9, 9½, 9½, 10 in), ending with a WS row.

Shape Shoulder and Back Neck

Whilst maintaining button border cast off 11 (12, 12, 12, 12, 13, 13, 13, 14, 14, 15) sts at beg of next and foll alt row. Place rem 29 (29, 32, 33, 33, 33, 35, 35, 36, 36, 36) sts on holder.

With RS facing, rejoin yarn to rem sts and commence working as folls:

Row 1 (RS): Sl1, K to end.

Row 2: P to end.

Rep these 2 rows until armhole measures 18½ (19, 21, 21, 22, 22, 23, 23, 24, 24, 25½) cm (7¼, 7½, 8¼, 8¼, 8½, 8½, 9, 9, 9½, 9½, 10 in), ending with a RS row.

Shape Shoulder and Back Neck

Cast off 11 (12, 12, 12, 12, 13, 13, 13, 14, 14, 15) sts at beg of next and foll alt row. Place rem 21 (21, 24, 25, 25, 25, 27, 27, 28, 28, 28) sts on holder.

FRONT

Work as for back until ***, 86 (90, 96, 98, 98, 102, 106, 106, 112, 112, 116) sts.

Work 1 row straight.

Row 1 (RS): K9 (11, 11, 12, 12, 14, 13, 13, 16, 16, 18), [P2, K4] 11 (11, 12, 12, 12, 12, 13, 13, 13, 13, 13) times, P2, K9 (11, 11, 12, 12, 14, 13, 13, 16, 16, 18).

Row 2: P9 (11, 11, 12, 12, 14, 13, 13, 16, 16, 18), K2, [P4, K2] 11 (11, 12, 12, 12, 12, 13, 13, 13, 13, 13) times, K2, P9 (11, 11, 12, 12, 14, 13, 13, 16, 16, 18).

Row 3: As row 1.

Row 4: As row 2.

Row 5: K9 (11, 11, 12, 12, 14, 13, 13, 16, 16, 18), [P2, TW4] 11 (11, 12, 12, 12, 12, 13, 13, 13, 13, 13) times, P2, K9 (11, 11, 12, 12, 14, 13, 13, 16, 16, 18).

Row 6: As row 2.

These 6 rows form patt. Work in patt as set until front measures 28 (28, 28, 30, 30, 30, 32, 32, 34, 34, 34) rows less than back to start of shoulder shaping.

Shape Neck

Continuing to work patt as set shape neck as folls:

Next row (RS): Patt 35 (37, 37, 38, 38, 40, 41, 41, 44, 44, 46), turn, placing rem sts on holder. Dec 1 st at neck edge of 13 (13, 13, 14, 14, 14, 15, 15, 16, 16, 16) foll alt rows, 22 (24, 24, 24, 24, 26, 26, 26, 28, 28, 30) sts.

Work 1 row straight, thus ending with a WS row.

Shape Shoulder

With RS facing, cast off 11 (12, 12, 12, 12, 13, 13, 13, 14, 14, 15) sts at beg of next and foll alt row.

Leaving centre 16 (16, 22, 22, 22, 22, 24, 24, 24, 24, 24) sts on holder, and with RS facing, rejoin yarn to rem sts and patt to end, 35 (37, 37, 38, 38, 40, 41, 41, 44, 44, 46) sts.

Dec 1 st at neck edge of 13 (13, 13, 14, 14, 14, 15, 15, 16, 16, 16) foll alt rows, thus ending with a RS row, 22 (24, 24, 24, 24, 26, 26, 26, 28, 28, 30) sts.

Shape Shoulder

With WS facing, cast off 11 (12, 12, 12, 12, 13, 13, 13, 14, 14, 15) sts at beg of next and foll alt row.

SLEEVES

Using 2.75mm needles cast on 58 (64, 72, 78, 86, 92, 100, 106, 114, 120, 128) sts and work in rib as folls:

Next row (RS): * K1, P1, rep from * to end.

Rep this row until work measures 5cm (2in) ending with a WS row.

Change to 3mm needles and commencing with a K row work in stocking stitch and AT THE SAME TIME inc 1 st at each end of 3rd and on every foll 4th (4th, 4th, 4th, 4th, 4th, 4th, –, –, 5th, 5th) row 4 (4, 4, 4, 4, 4, 4, 0, 0, 3, 5) times, 68 (74, 82, 88, 96, 102, 110, 108, 116, 128, 140) sts. Inc 1 st at each end of every foll 5th (5th, 5th, 5th, 5th, 5th, 5th, 5th, 5th, 6th, 6th) row 2 (2, 2, 2, 2, 2, 2, 6, 6, 3, 2) times, 72 (78, 86, 92, 100, 106, 114, 120, 128, 134, 144) sts.

Work without further shaping for 6 rows.

Shape Sleeve Head

Cast off 3 (3, 3, 4, 4, 4, 5, 5, 5, 6, 6) sts at beg of next 4 (4, 4, 4, 4, 4, 8, 8, 8, 8, 8) rows, 60 (66, 74, 76, 84, 90, 74, 80, 88, 86, 96) sts. Dec 1 st at each end of next and 5 (10, 14, 17, 27, 28, 14, 19, 27, 18, 29) foll alt rows, 48 (44, 44, 40, 28, 32, 44, 40, 32, 48, 36) sts.

6th size only

Then dec 1 st at each end of every row 4 times (24 sts).

All other sizes

Then dec 1 st at each end of every 3rd row 12 (10, 10, 8, 2, –, 10, 8, 4, 12, 6) times, (24 sts rem).

All sizes

Cast off rem sts.

MAKING UP

Press work lightly on WS of work through damp cloth. Do not press ribbing. Join shoulders.

NECK BAND

Using 2.75mm needles and with RS facing rejoin yarn and knit across 21 (21, 24, 25, 25, 25, 27, 27, 28, 28, 28) sts on left back, then pick up and K 18 (18, 18, 20, 20, 20, 20, 20, 24, 24, 24) sts down left front neck, K16 (16, 22, 22, 22, 22, 24, 24, 24, 24, 24) across front neck, pick up and K 18 (18, 18, 20, 20, 20, 20, 20, 24, 24, 24) sts up right front neck, then K across 21 (21, 24, 25, 25, 25, 27, 27, 28, 28, 28) sts on right back neck, patt 8 sts of button border, 102 (102, 114, 120, 120, 120, 126, 126, 136, 136, 136) sts.

Next row (WS): Patt 8 sts, * K1, P1, rep from * to end.
Next row: * K1, P1, rep from * to last 8 sts, patt to end.

Rep these 2 rows twice more (6 rows worked in total). Cast off in rib.

Sew up side and sleeve seams. Insert sleeve into armhole, taking care to match centre of sleeve head with shoulder seam. Lap button border at back neck over left centre back and slip stitch in place at cast on edge.

Darn in all ends. Sew 2 press studs in place on underside of button border, and sew 2 buttons on RS to cover if desired. Sew an additional press stud and button in position on rib band above border.

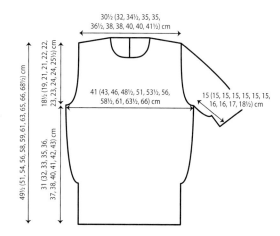

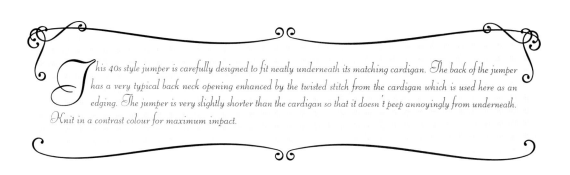

This 40s style jumper is carefully designed to fit neatly underneath its matching cardigan. The back of the jumper has a very typical back neck opening enhanced by the twisted stitch from the cardigan which is used here as an edging. The jumper is very slightly shorter than the cardigan so that it doesn't peep annoyingly from underneath. Knit in a contrast colour for maximum impact.

Embassy Gloves

MATERIALS

Eden Cottage Tempo 4 ply 75% wool / 25% nylon
(399m / 436yds per 100g skein)
1 skein shade Carnelian
1 set 2.75mm (US #2) double pointed needles (DPNs)
1 set 2.25mm (US #1) double pointed needles (DPNs)
Stitch markers
Waste yarn

TENSION

36 sts & 44 rows = 10cm (4in) using 2.75mm needles
measured over stocking stitch

ABBREVIATIONS

See page 95

SIZING

Medium Ladies – circumference around hand above thumb – 16cm (6¼in)
Large Ladies – circumference around hand above thumb – 19cm (7½in)

To make fingers fit exactly, place each hand on a piece of paper and draw round the hand to provide a template.
Then simply knit the glove digits until they are of the required length.

PATTERN NOTES

Central Leaf Pattern 15 sts (worked in the round)
This panel has 17 sts at the end of rows 1–4 and
15 sts at the end of all other rows.

Round 1: K1, YO, K5, YO, Sl1, K2tog, psso, YO, K5, YO, K1, 17 sts.
Round 2: K17.
Round 3: K1, YO, K1, K2tog, P1, Sl1, K1, psso, K1, YO, P1, YO, K1, K2tog, P1, Sl1, K1, psso, K1, YO, K1.
Round 4: K4, [P1, K3] twice, P1, K4.
Round 5: K1, YO, K1, K2tog, P1, Sl1, K1, psso, K1, P1, K1, K2tog, P1, Sl1, K1, psso, K1, YO, K1, 15 sts.
Round 6: K4, [P1, K2] twice, P1, K4.
Round 7: [K1, YO] twice, K2tog, P1, Sl1, K1, psso, P1, K2tog, P1, Sl1, K1, psso, [YO, K1] twice.
Round 8: K5, [P1, K1] twice, P1, K5.
Round 9: K1, YO, K3, YO, Sl1, K2tog, psso, P1, K3tog, YO, K3, YO, K1.
Round 10: K15.

These 10 rounds form pattern.

These gloves are worked from the cuff down, with a picot hem created at the top of the glove for the cuff. The Leaf pattern is worked across the centre front of the glove with the lace rib pattern worked over the remaining stitches. A small number of decreases are worked to create shaping at the lower arm but most of the shaping is created by changing down needle sizes at the lower arm. If you do not require lower arm shaping, simply work the pattern as written but do not change to smaller needles when suggested. The knitting is worked from the outer side seam position – in line with the little finger.

Both written and charted instructions are provided for the central Leaf panel. As the gloves are worked in the round the chart must be read from right to left on every round.

RIGHT GLOVE
Hem
Using 2.75mm needles, cast on 68 (80) sts using cable cast on, and join into a round, taking care not to twist stitches. Place marker at join.

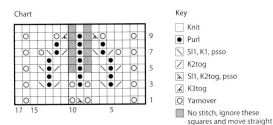

Chart

17	15		10		5			

9
7
5
3
1

Key

☐ Knit
● Purl
╲ Sl1, K1, psso
╱ K2tog
⋋ Sl1, K2tog, psso
⋌ K3tog
○ Yarnover
▨ No stitch, ignore these squares and move straight to next knitting instruction

K 4 rounds.

Next round (Picot): * YO, K2tog, rep from * to end of round.

K 4 rounds.

Next round (Hem): * K together first st from live sts with corresponding cast on st, rep from * to end. K 1 round.**

Place Pattern

Round 1 (Leaf panel inc): [YO, K2tog, K1] 2 (3) times, P2, work round 1 of leaf pattern, P2, [K1, YO, K2tog] 14 (17) times, K1, 70 (82) sts.

Round 2: [K2tog, YO, K1] 2 (3) times, P2, work round 2 of leaf pattern, P2, [K1, K2tog, YO] 14 (17) times, K1.

These 2 rounds set leaf pattern placement and lace rib pattern. Continue as set until all 10 rounds of leaf pattern have been worked.

Rep these 10 rounds a further 6 times, 68 (80) sts.

Lower Arm Shaping

Next round (Dec & leaf panel inc): [YO, K2tog, K1] 2 (3) times, P2tog, work round 1 of leaf pattern, P2tog, [K1, YO, K2tog] 14 (17) times, K1, 68 (80) sts.

Round 2: [K2tog, YO, K1] 2 (3) times, P1, work round 2 of leaf pattern, P1, [K1, K2tog, YO] 14 (17) times, K1.

Continue as now set, working only one P st at either side of leaf pattern until all 10 rounds of leaf pattern have been worked, 66 (78) sts.

Change to 2.25mm needles and work 10 rounds of patt twice more then change back to 2.75mm needles and work 10 rounds of patt 2 times more, followed by a further 8 (4) rounds of leaf pattern, 66 (80) sts. (158 (154) rounds of leaf pattern worked in total.)

Small size only

Next round (Thumb inc): [YO, K2tog, K1] 2 times, P1, work round 9 of leaf pattern, P1, K1, YO,

K2tog, M1, [K1, YO, K2tog] 5 times, M1, [K1, YO, K2tog] 8 times, K1, 68 sts.

Next round: [K2tog, YO, K1] 2 times, P1, work round 10 of leaf pattern, P1, K1, K2tog, YO, K2, K2tog, YO, [K1, K2tog, YO] 4 times, K2, K2tog, YO, [K1, K2tog, YO] 7 times, K1.

Large size only

Next round (Thumb inc, leaf panel dec): [YO, K2tog, K1] 3 times, P1, work round 5 of leaf pattern, P1, [K1, YO, K2tog] 2 times, M1, [K1, YO, K2tog] 5 times, M1, [K1, YO, K2tog] 10 times, K1, 80 sts.

Next round: [K2tog, YO, K1] 3 times, P1, work round 6 of leaf pattern, P1, [K1, K2tog, YO] 2 times, K1, [K1, K2tog, YO] 5 times, K1, [K1, K2tog, YO] 10 times, K1.

Next round (Thumb inc): [YO, K2tog, K1] 3 times, P1, work round 7 of leaf pattern, P1, [K1, YO, K2tog] 2 times, M1, K1, [K1, YO, K2tog] 5 times, K1, M1, [K1, YO, K2tog] 10 times, K1, 82 sts.

Next round: [K2tog, YO, K1] 3 times, P1, work round 8 of leaf pattern, P1, [K1, K2tog, YO] 2 times, K2, [K1, K2tog, YO] 5 times, K2, [K1, K2tog, YO] 10 times, K1.

Next round (Thumb inc): [YO, K2tog, K1] 3 times, P1, work round 9 of leaf pattern, P1, [K1, YO, K2tog] 2 times, M1, K2, [K1, YO, K2tog] 5 times, K2, M1, [K1, YO, K2tog] 10 times, K1, 84 sts.

Next round: [K2tog, YO, K1] 3 times, P1, work round 10 of leaf pattern, P1, [K1, K2tog, YO] 2 times, K3, [K1, K2tog, YO] 5 times, K3, [K1, K2tog, YO] 10 times, K1.

Divide for Thumb (Both sizes)

Next round (Leaf panel inc): [YO, K2tog, K1] 2 (3) times, P1, work round 1 of leaf pattern, P1, [K1, YO, K2tog] 1 (2) times, slip next 17 (21) sts onto waste yarn and leave to work thumb, cast on 6 sts, [K1, YO, K2tog] 8 (10) times, K1, 59 (71) sts.

Round 2: [K2tog, YO, K1] 2 (3) times, P1, work round 2 of leaf pattern, P1, [K1, K2tog, YO] 11 (14) times, K1.

Round 3: [YO, K2tog, K1] 2 (3) times, P1, work round 3 of leaf pattern, P1, [K1, YO, K2tog] 11 (14) times, K1.

Continue as now set until 2 leaf patt reps have been worked from thumb divide, 57 (69) sts.

From this point work in stocking stitch throughout – every round K.

First Finger (Index finger)
K37 (44) sts, place rem 20 (25) sts from palm of hand onto waste yarn, cast on 3 sts, P19 (22) and slip rem 21 (25) sts from back of hand onto waste yarn. Join finger sts into a round and K every round until finger is required length, 19 (22) sts.

Shape Top
Next round (Dec): [K1, K2tog] 6 (7) times, K1, 13 (15) sts.
Next round: K.
Next round: [K2tog] to last st, K1, 7 (8) sts.
Break yarn, draw through rem sts and fasten off securely.

Second Finger (Middle finger)
With back of hand (Leaf panel) facing slip 7 (8) sts nearest to first finger back onto needle, rejoin yarn and K across these sts, pick up and K 3 sts from base of first finger, slip next 7 (9) sts from palm of hand onto a second needle then K across these sts, cast on a further 3 sts and join finger into a round, 20 (23) sts.

K every round until finger is required length.

Shape Top
Next round (Dec): [K1, K2tog] 6 (7) times, K2, 14 (16) sts.
Next round: K.
Next round: [K2tog] to end, 7 (8) sts.
Break yarn, draw through rem sts and fasten off securely.

Third Finger (Ring finger)
With back of hand (Leaf panel) facing slip 7 (9) sts nearest to second finger back onto needle, rejoin yarn and K across these sts, pick up and K 3 sts from base of second finger, slip next 7 (8) sts from palm of hand onto a second needle then K across these sts, cast on a further 3 sts and join finger into a round, 20 (23) sts.

K every round until finger is required length.

Shape Top
Shape top as for second finger.

Fourth Finger (Little finger)
With back of hand (Leaf panel) facing slip rem 8 (8) sts nearest to third finger back onto needle, rejoin yarn and K across these sts, pick up and K 3 sts from base of third finger, slip rem 6 (8) sts from palm of hand onto a second needle then K across these sts. Join finger into a round, 16 (19) sts.

K every round until finger required length.

Shape Top
Next round (Dec): [K1, K2tog] 5 (6) times, K1, 11 (13) sts.
Next round: K.
Next round: [K2tog] 5 (6) times, K1, 6 (7) sts.
Break yarn, draw through rem sts and fasten off securely.

Thumb

Rejoin yarn to 17 (21) sts on waste yarn for thumb. Knit across these 17 (21) sts, pick up and knit 6 sts from cast on edge of hand. Join thumb into a round, 23 (27) sts.

K every round until thumb is required length.

Shape Top

Next round (Dec): [K1, K2tog] 7 (9) times, K2 (0), 16 (18) sts.
Next round: K.
Next round: [K2tog] 8 (9) times, 8 (9) sts.
Break yarn, draw through rem sts and fasten off securely.

LEFT GLOVE

Work as for right glove to **.

Place Pattern

Round 1 (Leaf panel inc): K1, [YO, K2tog, K1] 14 (17) times, P2, work round 1 of leaf pattern, P2, [K1, YO, K2tog] 2 (3) times, 70 (82) sts.
Round 2: K1, [K2tog, YO, K1] 14 (17) times, P2, work round 2 of leaf pattern, P2, [K1, K2tog, YO] 2 (3) times.

These 2 rounds set leaf pattern placement and lace rib pattern. Continue as set until all 10 rounds of leaf pattern have been worked.
Rep these 10 rounds a further 6 times, 68 (80) sts.

Lower Arm Shaping

Next round (Dec & leaf panel inc): K1, [YO, K2tog, K1] 14 (17) times, P2tog, work round 1 of leaf pattern, P2tog, [K1, YO, K2tog] 2 (3) times, 68 (80) sts.
Round 2: K1, [K2tog, YO, K1] 14 (17) times, P1, work round 2 of leaf pattern, P1, [K1, K2tog, YO] 2 (3) times.
Continue as now set, working only one P st at either side of leaf pattern until all 10 rounds of leaf pattern have been worked, 66 (78) sts.

Change to 2.25mm needles and work 10 rows of patt twice more then change back to 2.75mm needles and work 10 rows of patt 2 times more, followed by a further 8 (4) rounds of leaf pattern, 66 (80) sts. (158 (154) rounds of leaf pattern worked in total.)

Small size only

Next round (Thumb inc): K1, [YO, K2tog, K1] 8 times, M1, [YO, K2tog, K1] 5 times, M1, YO, K2tog, K1, P1, work round 9 of leaf pattern, P1, [K1, YO, K2tog] 2 times.
Next round: K1, [K2tog, YO, K1] 8 times, K1, [K2tog, YO, K1] 5 times, K1, K2tog, YO, K1, P1, work round 10 of leaf pattern, P1, [K1, K2tog, YO] 2 times.

Large size only

Next round (Thumb inc, leaf panel dec): K1, [YO, K2tog, K1] 10 times, M1, [YO, K2tog, K1] 5 times, M1, [YO, K2tog, K1] 2 times, P1, work round 5 of leaf pattern, P1, [K1, YO, K2tog] 3 times, 80 sts.
Next round: K1, [K2tog, YO, K1] 10 times, K1, [K2tog, YO, K1] 5 times, K1, [K2tog, YO, K1] 2 times, P1, work round 6 of leaf pattern, P1, [K1, K2tog, YO] 3 times.
Next round (Thumb inc): K1, [YO, K2tog, K1] 10 times, M1, K1, [YO, K2tog, K1] 5 times, K1, M1, [YO, K2tog, K1] 2 times, P1, work round 7 of leaf pattern, P1, [K1, YO, K2tog] 3 times, 82 sts.
Next round: K1, [K2tog, YO, K1] 10 times, K2,

[K2tog, YO, K1] 5 times, K2, [K2tog, YO, K1] 2 times, P1, work round 8 of leaf pattern, P1, [K1, K2tog, YO] 3 times.

Next round (Thumb inc): K1, [YO, K2tog, K1] 10 times, M1, K2, [YO, K2tog, K1] 5 times, K2, M1, [YO, K2tog, K1] 2 times, P1, work round 9 of leaf pattern, P1, [K1, YO, K2tog] 3 times, 84 sts.

Next round: K1, [K2tog, YO, K1] 10 times, K3, [K2tog, YO, K1] 5 times, K3, [K2tog, YO, K1] 2 times, P1, work round 10 of leaf pattern, P1, [K1, K2tog, YO] 3 times.

Divide for Thumb (Both sizes)

Round 1 (Leaf panel inc): K1, [YO, K2tog, K1] 8 (10) times, slip next 17 (21) sts onto waste yarn and leave to work thumb, cast on 6 sts, [YO, K2tog, K1] 1 (2) times, P1, work round 1 of leaf pattern, P1, [K1, YO, K2tog] 2 (3) times, 59 (71) sts.

Round 2: K1, [K2tog, YO, K1] 11 (14) times, P1, work round 2 of leaf pattern, P1, [K1, K2tog, YO] 2 (3) times.

Round 3: K1, [YO, K2tog, K1] 11 (14) times, P1, work round 3 of leaf pattern, P1, [K1, YO, K2tog] 2 (3) times.

Continue as now set until 2 leaf patt reps have been worked from thumb divide, 57 (69) sts.

From this point work in stocking stitch throughout – every round K.

First Finger (Index finger)

K36 (44) sts, place rem 21 (25) sts from back of hand onto waste yarn, cast on 3 sts, P19 (22) and slip rem 20 (25) sts from palm of hand onto waste yarn. Join finger sts into a round and K every round until finger is required length, 19 (22) sts. Complete first finger as for right glove.

Second Finger (Middle finger)

With palm of hand facing slip 7 (8) sts nearest to first finger back onto needle, rejoin yarn and K across these sts, pick up and K 3 sts from base of first finger, slip next 7 (9) sts from back of hand onto a second needle then K across these sts, cast on a further 3 sts and join finger into a round, 20 (23) sts. Complete second finger as for right glove.

Third Finger (Ring finger)

With palm of hand facing slip 7 (9) sts nearest to second finger back onto needle, rejoin yarn and K across these sts, pick up and K 3 sts from base of second finger, slip next 7 (8) sts from back of hand onto a second needle then K across these sts, cast on a further 3 sts and join finger into a round, 20 (23) sts. Complete third finger as for right glove.

Fourth Finger (Little finger)

With palm of hand facing slip rem 8 (8) sts nearest to third finger back onto needle, rejoin yarn and K across these sts, pick up and K 3 sts from base of third finger, slip rem 6 (8) sts from back of hand onto a second needle then K across these sts. Join finger into a round, 16 (19) sts.
Complete fourth finger as for right glove.

Complete thumb as for right glove.

MAKING UP
Darn in any ends. Press lightly.

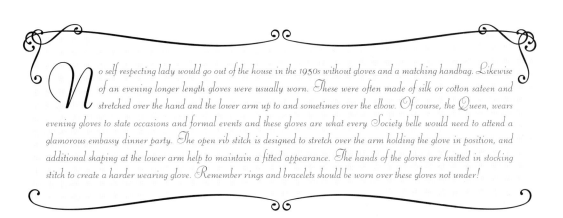

No self respecting lady would go out of the house in the 1950s without gloves and a matching handbag. Likewise of an evening longer length gloves were usually worn. These were often made of silk or cotton sateen and stretched over the hand and the lower arm up to and sometimes over the elbow. Of course, the Queen, wears evening gloves to state occasions and formal events and these gloves are what every Society belle would need to attend a glamorous embassy dinner party. The open rib stitch is designed to stretch over the arm holding the glove in position, and additional shaping at the lower arm help to maintain a fitted appearance. The hands of the gloves are knitted in stocking stitch to create a harder wearing glove. Remember rings and bracelets should be worn over these gloves not under!

Changing Guards at Buckingham Palace

MATERIALS

Jamieson & Smith 2 Ply Jumper weight 100% Shetland
wool (115m / 125yds per 25g ball)
4 (5, 7) balls shade 14 (blue) – MC
1 (1, 1) ball shade 1403 (red) – CC1
1 (1, 1) ball shade 01A (white) – CC2
1 (1, 1) ball shade 005 (black) – CC3

1 pair 2.75mm (US #2) needles
1 pair 3.25mm (US #3) needles
– or –
1 2.75mm (US #2) circular needle (60cm)
1 3.25mm (US #3) circular needle (60cm)
A set of 3.25mm (US #3) double pointed needles (DPNs)
or 1 3.25mm (US #3) circular needle (40cm long)

Waste yarn
Stitch markers
Spare needles
1 button
3mm crochet hook

TENSION

28 sts & 36 rows = 10cm (4in) using 3.25 needles
measured over stocking stitch

ABBREVIATIONS

See page 95

SIZING

Age		3–4	5–6	7–8
To Fit	cm	55–58½	60–63½	65–67
	(in)	(21½–23)	(23½–25)	(25½–26½)
Actual Chest Size	cm	60	68½	77
	(in)	(23½)	(27)	(30¼)
Length to Underarm	cm	25½	27½	32½
	(in)	(10)	(10¾)	(12¾)
Armhole Depth	cm	11½	12	13
	(in)	(4½)	(4¾)	(5)
Finished Length	cm	37	39½	45½
	(in)	(14½)	(15½)	(18)
Shoulder to Shoulder	cm	24½	25½	27
	(in)	(9½)	(10)	(10¾)

Size shown in photographs is to fit aged 3–4 years (chest size 55–58cm (21½–23in))

PATTERN NOTES

Pattern instructions are included to either knit this garment in the round or to knit the front and back as
separate pieces and then sew together.

Worked Flat

BACK

Cast on 84 (96, 108) sts using 2.75mm needles and MC and commence work as folls:

Next row: * K1, P1, rep from * to end.
Rep this row until rib measures 5cm (2in) ending with a WS row. Change to 3.25mm needles and commencing with a K row work in stocking stitch until work measures 7 (7½, 8) cm (2¾, 3, 3¼ in) ending with a WS row.

Row 1 (RS): Reading chart from right to left, repeat 12 stitch motif from row 1 of chart 7 (8, 9) times.

Row 2 (WS): Reading chart from left to right, repeat 12 stitch motif from row 2 of chart 7 (8, 9) times.

Continue as set until all 26 rows of chart completed.

Using MC only and commencing with a K row, work in stocking stitch until work measures 25½ (27½, 32½) cm (10, 11, 12¾ in) ending with a WS row. Please note, if preferred centre black stitch on row 12 can be swiss darned after knitting completed rather than working single black stitch on each motif. **

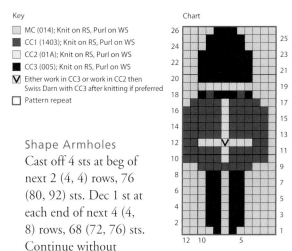

Key
- ▨ MC (014); Knit on RS, Purl on WS
- ▧ CC1 (1403); Knit on RS, Purl on WS
- ☐ CC2 (01A); Knit on RS, Purl on WS
- ■ CC3 (005); Knit on RS, Purl on WS
- ▽ Either work in CC3 or work in CC2 then Swiss Darn with CC3 after knitting if preferred
- ☐ Pattern repeat

Chart

Shape Armholes

Cast off 4 sts at beg of next 2 (4, 4) rows, 76 (80, 92) sts. Dec 1 st at each end of next 4 (4, 8) rows, 68 (72, 76) sts. Continue without further shaping until armhole measures 11½ (12, 13) cm (4½, 4¾, 5 in).

Shape Shoulders

Cast off 7 sts at beg of next 4 rows, 40 (44, 48) sts, then cast off 8 (9, 10) sts at beg of next 2 rows, 24 (26, 28) sts. Leave rem sts on holder.

FRONT

Work as for back to **.

Shape Armholes

Cast off 4 sts at beg of next 2 (4, 4) rows, 76 (80, 92) sts. Dec 1 st at each end of next 2 (0, 0) rows, 72 (80, 92) sts.

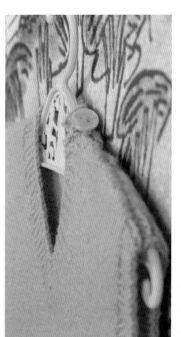

Shape Neck

Next row (RS): K2tog, K32 (36, 42), K2tog, turn, leaving rem 36 (40, 46) sts on holder, and patt to end, 34 (38, 44) sts.
Dec 1 st at armhole edge on foll 1 (3, 7) rows and AT THE SAME TIME, dec 1 st at neck edge on 11 (12, 13) foll 3rd rows, 22 (23, 24) sts.

Work without further shaping until piece measures same as back to start of shoulder shaping, ending with a WS row.

Shape Shoulder

Cast off 7 sts at beg of next and one foll alt row, 8 (9, 10) sts, then cast off 8 (9, 10) sts at beg of next alt row.

With RS facing rejoin yarn to rem 36 (40, 46) sts.
Next row: K2tog, K32 (36, 42), K2tog, 34 (38, 44) sts.
Dec 1 st at armhole edge on foll 1 (3, 7) rows and AT THE SAME TIME, dec 1 st at neck edge on 11 (12, 13) foll 3rd rows, 22 (23, 24) sts.

Work without further shaping until piece measures same as back to start of shoulder shaping, ending with a RS row.

Shape Shoulders

Cast off 7 sts at beg of next and one foll alt row, 8 (9, 10) sts, then cast off 8 (9, 10) sts at beg of next alt row.

MAKING UP

Swiss darn black buckle at centre of waist band if required. Press or block on WS of work. Darn in all ends. Sew right shoulder seam together.

NECK BAND

With RS facing, and using 3.25mm needles and MC, pick up and knit 29 (31, 33) sts down left front neck, pick up and knit 1 st at centre of V-neck, pick up and knit 29 (31, 33) sts up left front neck, K across 12 (13, 14) sts on back neck holder, M1, then K across rem 12 (13, 14) sts on holder at back neck, 84 (90, 96) sts.

Row 1 (WS): * K1 P1, rep to end, placing a marker either side of centre st.

Row 2 (RS): Rib to last st before first marker, Sl1, K2tog, psso, (move markers around this stitch), rib to end, 82 (88, 94) sts.

Row 3: Match rib as set.

Row 4: As row 2, 80 (86, 92) sts.

Row 5: As row 3.

Row 6: As row 2, 78 (84, 90) sts.

Row 7: As row 3.

Cast off loosely in rib to last st before marker, Sl1, K2tog, psso, then continue to cast off to end of row.

ARM BANDS

Sew left shoulder seam together, leaving neckband open.

With RS facing, and using 3.25mm needles and MC, pick up and knit 33 (34, 36) sts up first side of armhole to shoulder seam, then pick up and knit 33 (34, 36) sts down second side of armhole, 66 (68, 72) sts.

Next row (WS): * K1, P1, rep from * to end of row. Rep this row a further 5 times then cast off fairly loosely in rib.

Repeat for second armhole.

Join side seams. Darn in any remaining ends. Make a buttonhole loop on side edge of neckband as shown, using 3mm crochet hook and MC. Sew button onto facing edge of neckband to match.

Worked in the Round

Cast on 168 (192, 216) sts using 2.75mm circular needle and MC. Join into a round, taking care not to twist sts. Place marker at join (this marker denotes right seam position).

Round 1: * K1, P1, rep from * to end of round, placing marker after 84 (96, 108) sts have been worked.

Continue in rib as set until work measures 5cm (2in). Change to 3.25mm circular needle and K every round until work measures 7 (7½, 8) cm (2¾, 3, 3¼ in).

Next round: Reading from right to left, work row 1 of chart, repeating 12-stitch motif 14 (16, 18) times to end of round.

Continue working from chart, reading all rows from right to left, until all 26 rounds have been worked. Please note, if preferred centre black stitch on row 12 can be swiss darned after knitting completed rather than working single black stitch on each motif. Then using MC, K every round until work measures 25½ (27½, 32½) cm (10, 11, 12¾ in).

Divide for Armholes

Cast off 4 sts, K80 (92, 104), turn, cast off 4 and P76 (88, 100). Leave rem 84 (96, 108) sts on spare needle and continue on these 76 (88, 100) sts only, now working stocking stitch in rows.

UPPER BACK
Shape Armholes

2nd and 3rd sizes only
Cast off 4 sts at beg of next 2 rows (80, 92) sts.

All sizes
Commencing with a K row, dec 1 st at each end of every foll row 4 (4, 8) times, 68 (72, 76) sts. Work without further shaping until armhole measures 11½ (12, 13) cm (4½, 4¾, 5 in), ending with a WS row.

Shape Shoulders
K to last 7 sts, w&t,
P to last 7 sts, w&t
K to last 14 sts, w&t,
P to last 14 sts, w&t.
P8 (9, 10), then place both sets of 22 (23, 24)

shoulder sts on to spare needles, then place centre 24 (26, 28) sts on to stitch holder.

UPPER FRONT

The front will now be worked in stocking stitch in rows.

Return to rem 84 (96, 108) sts on spare needle. With RS facing, rejoin MC to rem sts and using 3.25mm needle, cast off 4 sts then K to end of row.

Next row (WS): Cast off 4 sts, P to end, 76 (88, 100) sts.

Shape Armholes

2nd and 3rd sizes only
Cast off 4 sts at beg of next 2 rows (80, 92) sts.

1st size only
Dec 1 st at each end of next 2 rows, 72 sts.

All sizes

Shape Neck

Next row (RS): K2tog, K32 (36, 42), K2tog, turn, leaving rem 36 (40, 46) sts on holder, and patt to end, 34 (38, 44) sts.
Dec 1 st at armhole edge on foll 1 (3, 7) rows and AT THE SAME TIME, dec 1 st at neck edge on 11 (12, 13) foll 3rd rows, 22 (23, 24) sts.

Work without further shaping until work measures same as back to start of shoulder shaping, ending with a RS row.

Shape Shoulder

P to last 7 sts, w&t,
K to end.
P to last 14 sts, w&t,
K to end.
Leave sts on holder.

With RS facing rejoin yarn to rem 36 (40, 46) sts.
Next row: K2tog, K32 (36, 42), K2tog, 34 (38, 44) sts.
Dec 1 st at armhole edge on foll 1 (3, 7) rows and AT THE SAME TIME, dec 1 st at neck edge on 11 (12, 13) foll 3rd rows, 22 (23, 24) sts.

Work without further shaping until work measures same as back to start of shoulder shaping, ending with a WS row.

Key

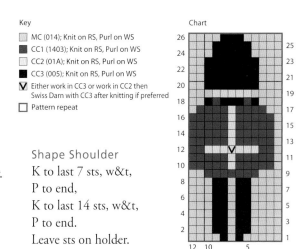

- ☐ MC (014); Knit on RS, Purl on WS
- ■ CC1 (1403); Knit on RS, Purl on WS
- ☐ CC2 (01A); Knit on RS, Purl on WS
- ■ CC3 (005); Knit on RS, Purl on WS
- ☑ Either work in CC3 or work in CC2 then Swiss Darn with CC3 after knitting if preferred
- ☐ Pattern repeat

Chart

Shape Shoulder

K to last 7 sts, w&t,
P to end,
K to last 14 sts, w&t,
P to end.
Leave sts on holder.

MAKING UP

Work three needle cast off to join shoulder seams, remembering to work each wrap together with corresponding wrapped st. If preferred, work one row on each shoulder prior to working cast off row, working wraps and wrapped sts together on this extra row.

Swiss darn black buckle at centre of waist band if required. Press or block on WS of work. Darn in all ends.

NECK BAND

With RS facing, and using 3.25mm DPNs or circular needles and MC, pick up and knit 29 (31, 33) sts down left front neck, pick up and knit 1 st at centre of V-neck, pick up and knit 29 (31, 33) sts up left front neck, K across 12 (13, 14) sts on back neck holder, M1, then K across rem 12 (13, 14) sts on holder at back neck, 84 (90, 96) sts. Neckband is now worked in rows to allow for neck opening.

Next row (WS): * K1 P1, rep to end, placing a marker either side of centre st.
Row 2: Rib to last st before first marker, Sl1, K2tog, psso, (move markers around this stitch), rib to end, 82 (88, 94) sts.
Row 3: Match rib as set.
Row 4: As row 2, 80 (86, 92) sts.
Row 5: As row 3.
Row 6: As row 2, 78 (84, 90) sts.
Row 7: As round 3.
Cast off loosely in rib to last st before marker, Sl1, K2tog, psso, then continue to cast off to end of row.

ARM BANDS

With RS facing, and using 3.25mm DPNs or a circular needle and MC, pick up and knit 33 (34, 36) sts up first side of armhole to shoulder seam, then pick up and knit 33 (34, 36) sts down second side of armhole, 66 (68, 72) sts. Place marker for end of round.

Next round (RS): * K1, P1, rep from * to end of rnd. Rep this round a further 5 times then cast off fairly loosely in rib.

Repeat on other armhole.

Make a buttonhole loop on side edge of neckband as shown, using 3mm crochet hook and MC. Sew button onto facing edge of neckband to match. Darn in any remaining ends.

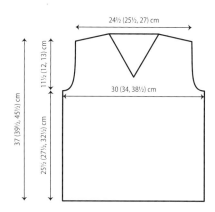

This little tank top or sleeveless pullover was inspired by the nursery rhyme by A A Milne – 'they're changing guards at Buckingham Palace, Christopher Robin went down with Alice' and a sweet little piece of ribbon I found with guardsmen embroidered in a long, long line along it. As soon as I drew my little guardsman on a piece of graph paper I was in love! The instructions for the pullover are provided both for it knitted flat in separate pieces or for it to be knitted in the round. The choice is yours. A tiny little bit of Swiss darning is needed to embroider on the guards' belt buckles. There are a number of occasions when more than two colours are used on any one row but as the guardsman motif is only worked over a few rows early on, all the hard work is out of the way at the beginning. I do think that a ladies cardigan with the same motif on may soon have to follow.

Blue Riband

MATERIALS
Babylonglegs Semi-Precious DK, 50% silk / 50% superwash merino (212m / 230yd per 100g skein)
1 skein, shade Feeling the Teal
Set of 4mm (US #6) double pointed needles (DPNs)
Stitch marker
½m (20in) of 1cm (½in) wide ribbon

TENSION
21 sts & 30 rows = 10cm (4in) using 4mm needles over stocking stitch (worked in the round)

ABBREVIATIONS
See page 95

SIZING
Circumference measured after brim shaping, but before crown shaping.

	cm	45½	51½	57
	(in)	(18)	(20)	(22½)
To fit size:	cm	45½	51½	57
	(in)	(18)	(20)	(22½)

PATTERN NOTES
This hat is knitted in the round from the bottom up, firstly by knitting a small hem. Short rows are worked at the back of the hat only to provide extra length for working tucks. If possible, use longer length dpns to provide enough room for the total number of stitches. Alternatively use a 60cm circular needle until too few stitches are left.

HAT
Using 4mm double pointed needles, cast on 108 (120, 132) sts onto one needle, then divide equally over three needles (36, 40, 44 sts on each). Join work into a round taking care not to twist stitches, placing stitch marker at join (this marks centre back) and commence working as folls:

Round 1: K.
Rounds 2 & 3: As round 1.
Round 4: P to form hem line.

K 3 rounds then commence short rows as folls:

Next round: K22 (26, 30) w&t.
Next round: P44 (52, 60) w&t.
Next round: K51 (59, 67) working wrap and wrapped st together, w&t.
Next round: P58 (66, 74) working wrap and wrapped st together, w&t.
Next round: K29 (33, 37) (end of round).
Next round: K108 (120, 132), working wraps and wrapped sts together.
K 16 rounds without further shaping.

Shape Brim
Round 30: * K16 (18, 20), K2tog, rep from * to end of round, 102 (114, 126) sts.
K 7 rounds.
Round 38: * K15 (17, 19), K2tog, rep from * to end of round, 96 (108, 120) sts.
K 7 rounds.

Shape Crown

Round 46: * K6 (7, 8), K2tog, rep from * to end of round, 84 (96, 108 sts).

K 5 rounds.

Round 52: * K5 (6, 7), K2tog, rep from * to end of round, 72 (84, 96 sts).

K 4 rounds.

Round 57: * K4 (5, 6), K2tog, rep from * to end of round, 60 (72, 84 sts).

K 3 rounds.

Round 61: * K3 (4, 5), K2tog, rep from * to end of round, 48 (60, 72 sts).

K 2 rounds.

Round 64: * K2 (3, 4), K2tog, rep from * to end of round, 36 (48, 60 sts).

K 1 round.

Round 66: * K4 (6, 8), K2tog, rep from * to end of round, 30 (42, 54 sts).

K 1 round.

Round 68: * K3 (5, 7), K2tog, rep from * to end of round, 24 (36, 48 sts).

K 1 round.

Round 70: * K2 (4, 6), K2tog, rep from * to end of round, 18 (30, 42 sts).

K 1 round.

Round 72: * K1 (3, 5), K2tog, rep from * to end of round, 12 (24, 36 sts).

1st size only

Break yarn and draw through remaining sts, fastening off securely.

2nd and 3rd sizes only

Now continue in this manner, decreasing 6 sts on each round, and working one st less between decs on every round, until (12, 18) sts remain.

Break yarn and draw through remaining sts, fastening off securely.

MAKING UP

Turn hem to WS at hem line, and with WS together pin then slip stitch loosely in place.

At centre back make three horizontal tucks as shown in photograph. Pin in position at centre back and then place a pin on lowest tuck 1cm at either side of centre pin, 2cm at either side of centre pin on second tuck, and 3cm at either side of centre pin on third tuck, thus creating folds. Once happy with positioning of tucks, catch stitch in place from WS of work at each of these points. Gather up tucks a little more on WS of work at centre back, fold ribbon in half at centre and pin in position on WS of hat over gathers at centre back. Slip stitch into place, then tie ribbon into bow at base of hat as shown.

Create ridge all around crown by creating a fold between 8th and 10th row from top of crown on RS of work. Pin all around and then using same yarn, work in running stitch right around this fold, thus making a permanent ridge as shown.

Darn in all ends. Place hat on head form or stuff with newspaper to create shape, then spray with a small amount of spray starch. Steam with a hot iron and then leave to dry.

The idea for this hat came from the archetypal face framing hats of the 1950s. Almost like a bonnet, they have a deep brim whilst the hat itself is designed to sit on the back of the head rather than on the top. I found a similar hat in a 1953 pattern book which I interpreted, re-wrote and re-knitted until I was happy with the overall shape and fit. A little touch of a decorative ribbon at the centre back of the hat gave me the idea for the name. I additionally love the fact that whilst the ribbon is decorative and makes a feature of the nape of the neck it also serves a function, reinforcing and holding together the folds created at the back of the hat. Short rows are worked to create added depth for the folds without interfering with the flattering shape at the front. Finally, spray starch is used to hold the hat's structure — alternatively you can dip your hat in sugar water if you want to be truly vintage!

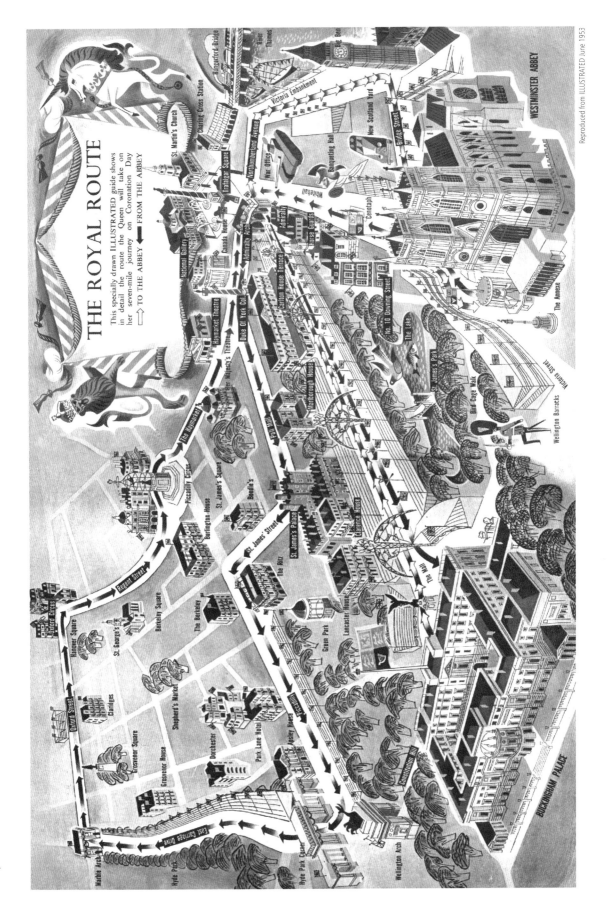

THE ROYAL ROUTE

This specially drawn ILLUSTRATED guide shows in detail the route the Queen will take on her seven-mile journey on Coronation Day

⟶ TO THE ABBEY ⬅ FROM THE ABBEY

Abbreviations

K – knit

P – purl

st(s) – stitch(es)

st st – stocking stitch

m – metres

yds – yards

cm – centimetres

in – inches

mm – millimetres

g – gram

DPNs – double pointed needles

MC – main colour

CC – contrast colour

LH – left hand

RH – right hand

RS – right side

WS – wrong side

Patt – pattern

Alt – alternate

Beg – beginning

Rep – repeat

rnd – round

Cont – continue

foll – following

folls – follows

rem – remaining

PM – place marker

SM – slip marker

Sl1 – slip one st (purlwise unless directed otherwise)

psso – pass slipped stitch over

YO – yarn over (also known as yarn forward or yarn round needle)

inc – increase (if used during an instruction ie. Inc 1 st, work either as Kfb or Pfb depending on how sts presented on needle)

dec – decrease, usually by knitting or purling two together

Kfb – knit into front and back of next stitch

Pfb – purl into front and back of next stitch

K2tog – knit two together

K3tog – knit three together

P2tog – purl two together

K2togtbl – knit two together through back of loops

P2togtbl – purl two together through back of loops

K3togtbl – knit three together through back of loops

M1 – make one, by knitting into loop lying between stitches

w&t – wrap and turn (see Knitting Know How on page 8)

Wfb – work into front and back of next st by purling into front then knitting into back of st before removing from left hand needle

SSK – slip next two stitches knitwise, then knit together through back of stitches

Sl1 pwise wyif – slip 1 stitch purlwise with yarn in front

2 stitches from 3 – Sl1, K1 leaving original st on left needle, pass slip st on right needle over new st now also on right needle, then knit stitch rem on left needle together with next st. This turns 3 stitches into two stitches.

TW4 – knit into front of 4th st on left hand needle, then before slipping it off needle, K 1st, 2nd then 3rd sts from left hand needle in turn, slipping 4th st off needle after 3rd st completed.

Slyo – slipped yarnover (see Knitting Know How on page 8).

T2 – Insert point of RH needle through first st on LH needle as though to purl. With needle in this position K next st on LH needle, drawing loop through both sts. Leave worked st on LH needle and knit into back of first st, slip both sts off LH needle.

K1A(B/C) – Knit 1 stitch using yarn A, B or C as stated.

About the Author

Susan Crawford is a British designer, author and fashion historian, specialising in vintage knitwear and with a range of publications and extensive experience in the knitting and fashion industry, is widely regarded as an expert in her craft. Susan's name has become synonymous with well executed designs that either draw inspiration from bygone days to create original pieces or re-interpret vintage patterns for a contemporary audience. Susan is a celebrated designer, stylist and publisher who is dedicated to authenticity and beauty. Coronation Knits is Susan's fourth book to date and builds on the success of her previous work which includes the highly acclaimed A Stitch In Time, Volumes 1 and 2.

Available from Susan Crawford

A Stitch in Time, Vol. 1
Vintage Knitting & Crochet
Patterns 1920-1949
Jane Waller & Susan Crawford

A Stitch in Time, Vol. 2
Vintage Knitting Patterns 1930-1959
Susan Crawford & Jane Waller

Vintage Gifts to Knit
Susan Crawford

Susan Crawford Vintage
www.susancrawfordvintage.com